EARTH'S EVENTIDE AND THE BRIGHT DAWN OF THE ETERNAL DAY

Published @ 2017 Trieste Publishing Pty Ltd

ISBN 9780649567133

Earth's Eventide and the Bright Dawn of the Eternal Day by J. G. Gregory

Edited by Trieste Publishing Pty Ltd.
Cover @ 2017

www.triestepublishing.com

J. G. GREGORY

EARTH'S EVENTIDE AND THE BRIGHT DAWN OF THE ETERNAL DAY

Trieste

EARTH'S EVENTIDE.

EARTH'S EVENTIDE

AND THE

Bright Dawn of the Eternal Day.

BY THE

REV. J. G. GREGORY, M.A.,

INCUMBENT OF EMMANUEL CHURCH, HOVE, BRIGHTON;
LATE MINISTER OF PARK CHAPEL, CHELSEA;
AND SOMETIME RECTOR OF BONCHURCH, ISLE OF WIGHT.

FIFTH EDITION.

LONDON:
S. W. PARTRIDGE & CO., 9, PATERNOSTER ROW.

MDCCCLXXX.

PREFACE .

———◆◇◆———

THE OUTLINES of the several subjects which are contained in this volume were arranged for, and delivered in the form of, "ADVENT LECTURES," in the years 1861 and 1862.

Having filled up these outlines with many details which appear to me important, I venture to commit them to the printer's hand, and thence to send them forth for the consideration of those Students of the Prophetical Scriptures who may be disposed to read them.

For adding thus to the already overwhelming mass of commentaries on the Word of God, it will be needful that I offer but this brief apology,—several Christian friends having heard the Lectures delivered, made request that I would publish them.

Conscious am I truly of defects, which the critic will discover readily. But let him not be too severe; let him believe, rather, that my object is the spiritual welfare of our fellow-Christians, and let him deal with me in that spirit of forbearance which such kind belief so readily begets.

And now, I pray Almighty God that He will give His blessing to this little work, and pardon all erroneous dealings with the deeper things of His Inspired Word. May He in mercy grant that both the writer and the reader, being strengthened by whatever has been written in accordance with His Will, may be guided safely through the trying periods which remain of this "Earth's Eventide," and be led onwards to the dawning of that glorious Day in which the servants of the Lord who have been waiting for His Advent shall shine forth in brightness like the Sun, and dwell before the throne of the eternal King of kings, in THE UNCEASING GLORY OF THE NEW JERUSALEM.

J. G. GREGORY.

BONCHURCH RECTORY :
   April, 1863.

PREFACE

————◦◦◦————

IN issuing the Fifth Edition of this little Work, I cannot help expressing a sincere feeling of thankfulness that I am enabled, by the continued demand for the book, to feel justified in laying it again before the Christian Church.

I have not found it necessary to alter the substance of any prophetical interpretation which the former Editions advanced. The matter of the book and the arrangement of the subjects are the same. The few alterations in this Edition are only such as the progress of events, during the seventeen years which have elapsed since the first Edition was published, has rendered necessary for the better comprehension of those who read from the standpoint of 1880 the pages which were written in 1863.

May the Lord continue His blessing upon the feeble effort of His servant, glorify His name, and advance the interests of His kingdom.

J. G. GREGORY.

112, LANSDOWNE PLACE,
HOVE, BRIGHTON.
June, 1880.

CONTENTS.

———•○•———

CHAPTER IV.

The Advent CII

CHAPTER V.

The Judgment of the Nations . . CXXX

CHAPTER VI.

CHAPTER VII.

CHAPTER VIII.

CHAPTER IX.

CHAPTER X.

EARTH'S EVENTIDE

Introductory Chapter.

"We have also a more sure word of Prophecy; whereunto ye do well that ye take heed, as unto a light that shineth in a dark place, until the day dawn, and the day star arise in your hearts."   2 PETER i. 19.

WE are told on every side that we are living in remarkable times. We read of it in the newspapers; we hear of it in our daily conversation; and we feel it to be true. There are undoubtedly the tokens of some extraordinary earthquake, which, growing more and more distinct, forewarn the thoughtful that a crisis of no slight importance is not far in our advance. We see, indeed, the Christian, the unbeliever, the philanthropist, and the politician, agreeing together in the expectation of some gigantic outburst. We find the hearts of men of judgment "failing them for fear, and for looking after those things which are coming on the earth." The eyes of many turn with anxious gaze

towards the observers of the times, the learned, the
statesman, the merchants, and the ministers of the
Gospel, with the inquiry—"Watchman, what of the
night?" And who among the sons of men can satisfy
the inquiry? Opinions, various enough, come forth.
A rush of many voices gives reply. But who is to be
trusted? The only safe response which any man can
give, is this—"It is not for you to know the times and
the seasons which the Father hath put in His own
power." Yet, for all this, there is a ray of light, feeble
certainly, but not to be neglected, for it comes down
directly from that Father's hand of love, and sheds its
gentle beam upon this wondrous period in which we live.
By this *one* beam those men who have the Spirit of the
Lord can read a word of warning which diffuses joyful
expectation through their willing hearts. That word
is, "WATCH AND PRAY, FOR THE COMING OF THE LORD
DRAWS NEAR." This ray of light illuminates, moreover, a few *signs* and *portents*, and exhorts, "WHEN
THESE THINGS BEGIN TO COME TO PASS, LOOK UP, AND
LIFT UP YOUR HEADS; FOR YOUR REDEMPTION DRAWETH
NIGH."[1] Now for this little gleam, let us who know
the Saviour render praise; and while we read, and
watch, and pray, be humble, looking to the Lord
submissively, with patient, waiting hearts; behaving

Luke xxi. 28.

ourselves always circumspectly; being well prepared to leave this lower world, whenever our Redeemer's voice shall call us to arise and meet Him.

I know that there are Christians, not a few, who will agree that these are times which ought to lead God's people to be much upon the watch-tower, forasmuch as many things betoken clearly that the coming of the Lord is near. And doubtless there are others who, although, perhaps, they will not go so far as this, will yet agree that these are days when things around forbode a crisis which has scarcely known a precedent; I therefore confidently ask for the attention of my brethren in Christ, to the *heart-stirring* and *important* subject of those prophecies which concern THE FUTURE OF OUR WORLD, and cast a special light upon the SECOND ADVENT OF OUR LORD AND SAVIOUR.

Inasmuch as these prophecies have been, until of late years, studied by comparatively few, even among really Christian people, I ought, perhaps, before speaking directly upon the subject, to note carefully THE DUTY which unquestionably lies upon every one of us, to give them *an attention just as close as that we should afford to any other part of Holy Scripture.*

To this duty our attention is called by the text which heads this chapter. Let us observe its language. The ' WORD OF PROPHECY " of which it speaks (as we are informed by the twentieth verse), is contained in "THE SCRIPTURES." It is called a "SURE WORD OF PROPHECY;" MORE sure (as the context also shows us) than the word which the apostle spoke when they "made known the power and coming of our Lord Jesus Christ, though they had been eye-witnesses of His Majesty."[1] Again, it is compared to "a light that shineth in a dark place;" wherefore also the Lord's people are expressly told that they "DO WELL," that they "TAKE HEED" to it. And this, not just *occasionally*, but "UNTIL THE DAY DAWN, AND THE DAY STAR ARISE IN THEIR HEARTS."

With this text then for a witness, let us behold the Prophecies of Scripture as "A SURE WORD" on which we may repose our confidence; not as they are deemed by some, a word to be *laid by* at once, as *highly figurative* and *incomprehensibly mysterious*; unfit, therefore, for profitable study. Let us view them as a LIGHT sent for the illumination of the sincere inquirer, to be used as a continual guide by the Lord's earnest servants while they sojourn in the "dark place" of this life's pilgrimage; and let us avail ourselves unceasingly of their much-needed beams, until the night which is "far spent" shall pass away, and the great "day" of light and life so long foretold, shall "dawn."

But it may be asked—"Is it not *unduly inquisitive*,

[1] 2 Pet. i. 16.

and therefore wrong, to search out the momentous matters
which are yet before us in the future? Does not the
Lord intend rather that the prophecies should be studied
after the events which they predict have transpired, so that
His truth may be confirmed, and His faithfulness made
known? This is an objection which lays firm hold
upon the minds of not a few; so that we continually
hear it said, that while *fulfilled* prophecy is of great
utility, proving beyond controversy the fore-knowledge,
power, judgment, mercy, and deity of God, *unfulfilled*
prophecy had far better be passed over for the present,
lest we be found sinfully prying into those secret things
which belong only to the Lord. In reply to this, we
may again refer to the language of the same passage of
Scripture. The light of prophecy there spoken of, and
to which it is said we "do well that we take heed," is
not certainly a light prepared by God to cast its beams
upon the path in which a man *has* trodden *hitherto :* for,
mark the language—"Whereunto ye do well that ye
take heed, as unto a light that shineth in a dark place,
UNTIL THE DAY DAWN." This surely speaks with plainness. It is a light which shines as from a guiding lamp,
to show the traveller *where he is*, and *what is before him*.
Bishop Newton says that the Apostle Peter "is asserting and establishing the truth of Christ's second coming
in power and great glory. (*For we have not followed*

*cunningly devised fables, when we made known unto you
the power and coming of our Lord Jesus Christ, but were
eye-witnesses of His majesty.)*   *One* illustrious proof of
His coming in power and glory was His appearing in
glory and majesty at His transfiguration.   (*For He
received from God the Father honour and glory, when there
came such a voice to Him from the excellent glory—This
is my beloved Son, in whom I am well pleased—and this
voice which came from Heaven we heard when we were with
Him in the Holy Mount.)*   His appearing once in power
and great glory is a good argument that He *may* appear
again in like manner; and that He not only *may* but
WILL, we have the further assurance of PROPHECY; (*We
have also a more sure word of Prophecy, whereunto ye do
well that ye take heed.)"*

With the testimony of a Scholar and Divine so able,
we might well rest satisfied, even were the connexion in
which the passage stands less plain; and be confident
that the "sure word of Prophecy" before us, is a word
which has its great concern with *an important future;*
even with THAT DAY OF WONDERS WHEN THE GREAT
"REDEEMER SHALL RETURN AND COME TO ZION" TO
BE GLORIFIED OF ALL.   But it is not only this one
passage, with its surrounding context, which gives evidence that we "do well that we take heed" to the "sure
word of Prophecy" with reference to things to come.

We must take notice also of the words of Him whose name is "Truth." What could our Saviour mean but to advise His people thus, when He said, "There shall be signs in the sun, and in the moon, and in the stars, and upon the earth distress of nations with perplexity; the sea and the waves roaring; men's hearts failing them for fear, and for looking after those things which are coming on the earth. . . . When these things BEGIN to come to pass, then look up, and lift up your heads; for your redemption draweth nigh!"[1] What could our Saviour mean when He spoke these words, but to warn His disciples both of *that* day and *this*, and to teach them to look forward, marking well the signs of the times, that they might perceive clearly the approach of that glorious period to which He taught them to look forward? It *could* not be that they might profit thereby *after* the event—*after* the Lord's coming—*after* they should have received the inheritance. It *must* have been that they might be *in readiness*, with their loins girt about, and their lamps burning, and they themselves like servants watching for their Lord. I have read somewhere much as follows: "If the use of unfulfilled prophecy be *after* the event which it foretels has come to pass, it must be either to the *Lord's people* or to *wicked people* that it is found useful. Now, it *cannot* be of any

[1] Luke xxi. 25, 28.

use to the *wicked* : it must needs be *too late* to be of use to them, when its predictions have received accomplishment in their destruction.   The flood proved the truth of the Lord's word which Noah delivered ; but it certainly was too late to be of any use to the *wicked people* to whom Noah preached : and the *Lord's servants* had *no need* of such a proof as the fulfilment of the prophecy afforded, for they were well aware beforetime that God spoke in faithfulness and truth.   Moreover the wicked perished in the flood *because they did not believe the prophecy* BEFORE *its accomplishment,* and the family of Noah were only saved *because they did believe it."*

Surely, then, as the inspired John declares concerning the Apocalypse, so we may assert respecting every other prophecy which the Word of God brings forward, "Blessed is he that readeth, and they that hear the words of this Prophecy, and keep those things which are written therein."[1]   So reading and so hearing we shall not fall under the condemnation of the Jews of old—" Ye hypocrites ! ye can discern the face of the sky and of the earth; but how is it that ye do not discern this time ?"[2]

The objection, then, which many have advanced upon the ground of *undue inquisitiveness,* is idle.

---

[1] Rev. i. 3.   [2] Luke xii. 56.

Another objection is raised by many good and seriously-minded Christians. "Do but observe," they say, "how great is the number of those students of the unfulfilled prophecies who have made shipwreck! Moreover, see the differences which exist among those students who still stand their ground! Surely such a dangerous, or at least unsatisfactory subject ought to be avoided." Now, allowing that many have made shipwreck, and allowing that great differences of interpretation do exist (though I cannot altogether receive the statement as correct), surely prophecy is *not the only subject of great moment* which has become a stumbling-block, or concerning which there have been serious differences of opinion. Satan has been very busy in spreading error with regard to *every* spiritual matter, and his work has told with fearful power on many who were looked upon as the Lord's people. Indeed, the very GOSPEL OF SALVATION, which a man must needs receive or perish everlastingly, has been made a theme of study by vast numbers who have lacked the Spirit of the Lord, and so has proved "an instrument of destruction!"

But shall the Gospel, therefore, be a subject we forbid? Shall we keep it from our less learned brethren, our families, our neighbours, our poor? Surely not; for where can be the cause for fear as to those students of the Word who read with humble, self-distrustful hearts, since God has promised that He "will give His Holy Spirit unto them that ask Him?"[1]   "If any man lack wisdom let him ask of God, who giveth to all men liberally, and upbraideth not, and it shall be given him: but let him ask in faith, nothing wavering."[2]   So, let us conclude that there is help at hand; and when God plainly tells us—"Search the Scriptures:"[3]   "All Scripture is given by inspiration of God, and is profitable . . . that the man of God may be perfect:"[4] "Blessed is he that readeth and they that hear the words of this Prophecy:"[5]   "We have a more sure word of Prophecy, whereunto ye do well that ye take heed:"—we are not to shrink back, saying, as it were, "Lord, there are many parts of Scripture I am afraid to study, lest I may be led thereby to error;" but rather, WE ARE TO DO THAT WHICH HE HAS BIDDEN, WITHOUT GAINSAYING, and avail ourselves with gratitude of the high privilege which in His Word He offers us.

So far, then, for this objection also.   And now, if no antagonist *more powerful* than these arise (and I know of none more powerful), we may, beyond a doubt, decide that it is our BOUNDEN DUTY, as those servants who await their Lord's return, to study UNFULFILLED PRO-PHECY, as well as every other part of Holy Scripture.

[1] Luke xi 13.   [2] James i. 5, 6.   [3] John v. 39.
[4] 2 Tim. iii. 16, 17.   [5] Rev. i. 3.

It will not be right for me to quit the subject of this duty without adding a few serious words as to the MANNER in which the study of unfulfilled prophecy should be conducted.

The students of prophecy are actuated by a diversity of motives. Some study to obtain food for an imaginative fancy. None are more likely than these to reap error; for the object of God's Word is not to feast the imagination, but to save, establish, and comfort the immortal soul. Others study for the enjoyment of sublime language and splendid imagery, of which the inspired prophecies are full. These also are unlikely to arrive at truth; for God did not give His Word to gratify the taste, but to edify the spirit.

But we must not fail to note that there are also those who read and study meekly, prayerfully, and with a view to obtain instruction in such things as God has deemed it right to offer for the contemplation of His people; so that they may be in readiness when the great day of God approaches, and "be found worthy to escape those things which are coming upon the earth, and to stand before the Son of Man." [1] Such students have a blessing. They will be instructed by the Spirit: as it is written, "They shall all be taught of God;" [2]

---

[1] Luke xxi. 36.   [2] John vi. 45.

and they will not be allowed to fall into errors which might damage their eternal interests.

Still it cannot but be noticed with regret, that the attitude which is assumed by some of the more careful and sincere students of the prophecies is anything but seemly for poor erring mortals, when they deal with the deep mysteries of God. We find them making *positive assertions* as to things which are still veiled from human sight; advancing questionable theories, and adhering to them as if in all the world there were no men of judgment to be found, themselves excepted; dealing with prophetic symbols, dates, and parables, with a positiveness which savours not by any means of Christian humility.

Now let us not act like them; but rather, while we never shrink from reading, hearing, or studying *any portion* of God's Word, which He has given for our learning; while we use that Word in all its parts— histories, psalms, laws, gospel, and *prophecies ;* while we observe prophetic *images, symbols, parables,* and *dates ;* let us not dare, in any case which bears upon the future, to assert with positiveness that at such and such a time *this incident* or *that* shall come to pass; unless, indeed, we have *no room* for doubt by reason of the plainness of expression God has used concerning it. Such plainness of expression with regard to the prophetic *dates,* however, nowhere, I believe, occurs; but rather, with regard to every incident *yet future*, it is clearly intimated that "Of that day and that hour knoweth no man."[1] The time *may* come, and perhaps is *near at hand already*, when we shall be in a position to use the mysterious periods both of Daniel and the Apocalypse with greater certainty.[2] But for the present, although (as we shall see as we advance with our subject) they are of *great utility* to the waiting and watching Christian, yet we cannot, with anything like certainty, determine their respective limits.

Avoiding, then, *all positive assertion* as to such things as are still in mystery; let us use whatever God has put before us in those Holy Scriptures He has given for our learning, with all humility and reverence, keeping the great precept ever on our mind, viz., "Let your loins be girt about, and your lights burning, and ye yourselves like unto men that wait for their Lord."[3]

It now remains that I lay before you a brief outline of the subjects to be treated.

I shall confine myself to those predictions which relate distinctly to the Second Advent of the Lord Jesus Christ, His kingdom, and His people's glory; noting

---

[1] Matt. xxiv. 36; Mark xiii. 32, 33.
[2] Compare Dan. xii. 9, with Rev. xxii. 10.   [3] Luke xii. 35.

those points more especially which call upon the servants
of the Lord to watch and pray.

The GENERAL ORDER of our subjects will be as
follows :—

    THE STATE OF THE WORLD AND THE CHURCH WHEN
        THE COMING OF THE LORD DRAWS NEAR.
    ISRAEL AND ANTICHRIST.
    THE ADVENT.
    THE JUDGMENT OF THE NATIONS.
    THE REIGN OF PEACE.
    THE FINAL OUTBREAK OF EVIL.
    THE GENERAL RESURRECTION OF THE WICKED.
    THE NEW JERUSALEM.

Perhaps to some among my Christian brethren such
a catalogue of subjects bearing upon the Second Advent
of our Saviour may seem strange. They have been used
to look for a great Day of Judgment to burst suddenly
upon the world, in the brief twelve or four and twenty
hours of which, all things which appertain to earth are
to be brought quickly to an end: the heavens to pass
away; the elements to melt; the earth to be burned up;
the dead to be raised; the living to be changed; the
whole innumerable multitude to rise from out of the
midst of the tremendous wreck of nature, and to stand
above, in heights unknown, before the Son of Man, that

they may there and then be judged, and that upon each soul a sentence may be passed for weal or woe; which being done, the wicked are to go forth accordingly, to the eternal flames of hell, and the righteous into everlasting happiness.

It will be my endeavour to look very carefully into Scripture upon the subjects which will come before us. I will ask my fellow Christians to bear kindly with me if my views do not agree with theirs, and to follow me from passage to passage of the Word of God with patience, while I deal, as briefly as I can, consistently with clearness, upon these most important matters.

And now let me entreat those brethren who do look for the appearing of our Lord to pray that He will influence the whole Church by His Holy Spirit's teaching, so that all who believe in His Name may be found in the happy attitude of prepared expectation, ready to uplift as with one voice the words foretold, "Lo! THIS IS OUR GOD; WE HAVE WAITED FOR HIM, AND HE WILL SAVE US: THIS IS THE LORD; WE HAVE WAITED FOR HIM, WE WILL BE GLAD AND REJOICE IN HIS SALVATION."

CHAPTER II.

The World and the Church.

———•◇•———

" Take heed to yourselves, lest at any time your hearts be overcharged with
surfeiting, and drunkenness, and cares of this life, and so that day come
upon you unawares. For as a snare it shall come on all them that
dwell on the face of the whole earth. Watch ye therefore, and pray
always, that ye may be accounted worthy to escape all these things
that shall come to pass, and to stand before the Son of man."

LUKE xxi. 34-36.

———•◇•———

IN the Introductory Chapter I endeavoured to
establish the duty of studying the unfulfilled
prophecies, and to set forth the manner in
which such study should be carried on. I also laid
down the general scheme, upon the details of which I
will now enter.

THE CONDITION OF THE WORLD AND THE CHURCH
AS THE ADVENT OF OUR LORD APPROACHES will first
occupy our attention.

An idea is abroad in Christian society that through
the progress of civilization, and the gradual spread of
the Gospel, a Millennium of peace and righteousness

will be introduced, and this world will thereby be prepared for the Second Advent of our Lord. This is,
without doubt, a grand theory, and one which is sure
to obtain favour; but it is FALSE. A brief consideration
of our own times will, perhaps, aid us in arriving at
the truth concerning this. We live in days when science
and civilization have arrived at wondrous heights. Men's
talents were never so highly tutored; human skill was
never so developed: refinement also has attained to
exquisite perfection in almost every grade of life. But
what of PEACE? It is needful to speak very cautiously
respecting it, and to give all our science a direction
which concerns the munitions of war. And what of
RIGHTEOUSNESS? In every circle of society (clothed
indeed in seemly garment, but all the more iniquitous
by consequence) *ungodliness abounds: Sin* grows in presumption, and comes in with gentleness and plausibility,
to take possession and to overthrow. Surely we are
not making progress towards this visionary excellence.
Nay, but it would seem that we are departing further
day by day from what is good and holy. I need not
surely stay to offer proofs. The facts are patent to the
most casual observers of the times. No one who mingles
with society, or reads the daily newspapers, can help
lamenting that the case is *even thus.*

Let us look, now, at our Bibles, that we may know

assuredly what we must expect as time flies on, and the great day of Christ approaches.

In the first place, we find that nothing is laid down in plainer terms than that " iniquity shall abound " in a peculiar and fearful manner as the time draws near.

Our SAVIOUR's words are powerful, which in the twenty-fourth chapter of St. Matthew, and elsewhere, foretel some of the wonders of that " end " for which we look. He cheers us, indeed, by the declaration that " The Gospel of the kingdom shall be preached in all the world for a witness unto all nations," and by other gladdening assurances: but then, on the other hand, He forewarns us how that as the end draws near, "iniquity shall abound," and "the love of many shall wax cold." He reminds us of the days of NOAH, when the world was totally regardless of the fear of God, and when " every imagination of the thoughts of man's heart was only evil continually,"[1] and tells us, " So shall it be also in the days of the Son of Man."[2] He refers, likewise, to the days of LOT, when men were "sinners before the Lord exceedingly,"[3] and declares, "Even thus shall it be in the day when the Son of Man is revealed."[4] Elsewhere, too, we find Him asking the conclusive question, " Nevertheless, when the Son of Man cometh, shall He find faith on the earth ? "[5]

---

[1] Gen. vi. 5.   [2] Luke xvii. 26.   [3] Gen. xiii. 13.
          [4] Luke xvii. 30.   [5] Luke xviii. 8.

Observe also what the word of the APOSTLE PAUL was upon this subject. In his Second Epistle to the Thessalonians he warns us: "Let no man deceive you by any means, for that day shall not come, except there come a falling away first, and that Man of Sin be revealed, the Son of Perdition . . . . whom the Lord shall consume with the Spirit of His mouth, and shall destroy with the brightness of His coming. Even him, whose coming is after the working of Satan, with all power, and signs, and lying wonders, and with all deceivableness of unrighteousness in them that perish; because they received not the love of the truth, that they might be saved."[1] So likewise, in his Second Epistle to Timothy, we find him speaking of the "perilous times" which shall come "in the last days," when "men shall be lovers of their own selves, covetous, boasters, proud, blasphemers, disobedient to parents, unthankful, unholy, without natural affection, truce-breakers, false accusers, incontinent, fierce, despisers of those that are good, traitors, heady, high-minded, lovers of pleasure more than lovers of God; having a form of godliness, but denying the power thereof."[2] JUDE, also, in his short Epistle, warns us how that in the last time there shall be "mockers" who shall walk "after

[1] 2 Thess. ii. 3–10.   [2] 2 Tim. iii. 1–5.

their own ungodly lusts."[1] We are led to the same conclusion by the Book of Revelation.[2]

But if the evidence be so strong in the *New* Testament, we may expect to find some intimation of the same in the *Old* Testament also, since that part of the Inspired Word dwells likewise very fully on the subject of the Second Advent.

The ancient writers had *by no means* been permitted to lose sight of a matter so important. When Isaiah speaks so strongly of the final judgments which shall come upon the earth, *making it empty—laying it waste —turning it upside down—defiling it under the inhabitants thereof;*—what is the great cause assigned but that men "*have transgressed the laws, changed the ordinances, broken the everlasting covenant!*" "*Therefore* hath the curse devoured the earth, ... fear, and the pit, and the snare," are upon its inhabitants; it shall be "moved exceedingly, ... reel to and fro like a drunkard, and be removed, like a cottage, and the transgression thereof shall be heavy upon it."[3] Again, in speaking of the judgments which shall accompany the introduction of that day, when "the wolf and the lamb shall feed together, and the lion shall eat straw like the bullock," and "they shall not hurt nor destroy," he says, "Behold, the Lord will come with fire and with His chariots like

---

[1] Jude 18.   [2] Rev. xvi., xvii. xix., etc.   [3] Isa. xxiv. 6-22.

Foolscap 8vo., Cloth, Bevelled.   Price Eighteenpence.
With Engravings.

INTO THE LIGHT.

" Light, from whose rays all beauty springs."

By JENNIE PERRETT,

Author of " Ben Owen, a Lancashire Story."

CONTENTS.

LONDON :

S. W. PARTRIDGE & Co., 9, Paternoster Row.

a whirlwind, to render His anger with fury, and His rebuke with flames of fire; for by fire, and by His sword will the Lord plead with all flesh, and the slain of the Lord shall be many. . . . *For I know their works and their thoughts.* It shall come that I will gather all nations and tongues, and they shall come and see My glory. . . . And they shall go forth, and look upon the *carcases of the men that have transgressed against Me:* for their worm shall not die, neither shall their fire be quenched, and they shall be an abhorring unto all flesh."[1]

Refer also to the prophet DANIEL. In the seventh chapter we have the four great kingdoms of the world's history brought before us : the *fourth* enduring till the day when the judgment shall sit, and the saints of the Most High shall take the reins of government. We observe in reading this chapter that, although through wickedness each of these kingdoms was to meet with its destruction, the iniquity of *the fourth* is expressly dwelt upon, and it is declared that the sinfulness of this kingdom shall *not abate* until " *the judgment shall be set, and the books opened.*"[2] Of the last head of this kingdom it is declared, "He shall speak great words against the Most High, and shall wear out the saints of the Most High, and think to change times and laws; and

[1] Isa. lxvi. 15-24.   [2] Dan. vii. 10.

D

they shall be given into His hand, until a time, and times, and the dividing of time." And then it is added, "But the judgment shall sit, and they shall take away his dominion, to consume and to destroy it unto the end."[1] But let me ask you carefully to study the seventh, eighth, ninth, and eleventh chapters of this prophecy; and you will, I think, see clearly that as the time of the millennial reign approaches, we are to expect *wickedness to abound, and practise, and prosper,* with a mighty hand.

The glorious rest, therefore, which this world shall enjoy will not be *gradually developed :* it will not be brought about by education, nor by the preaching of the Gospel, nor by the mutual consent of nations, nor by any instrumentality whatsoever which mankind will set on foot. " *The whole world lieth in wickedness."* It *has* so lain since Adam fell. It *will* so lie until the day of its regeneration. And as we approach that day, the word will be heard with an increasing power, saying, "Woe to the inhabiters of the earth, and of the sea! for the devil is come down unto you, having great wrath, because he knoweth that he hath but a short time."[2]

But further. There shall be a PERIOD OF TRIBU-LATION such as has not been "since the beginning of the world."

---

[1] Dan. vii. 23-26.   [2] Rev. xii. 12.

I know not how to choose from the mass of Scripture passages which speak of those tremendous trials of the last days which will be the fit accompaniments of the increasing wickedness. The LORD, as Isaiah prophesied, "will punish the world for their evil, and the wicked for their iniquity, . . . I will cause the arrogancy of the proud to cease, and will lay low the haughtiness of the terrible. I will make a man more precious than fine gold; even a man than the golden wedge of Ophir. Therefore, I will shake the heavens; and the earth shall remove out of her place, in the wrath of the Lord of Hosts, and in the day of His fierce anger."[1] "Come near, ye nations, to hear; and hearken, ye people: let the earth hear, and all that is therein; the world, and all things that come forth of it. For the indignation of the Lord is upon all nations, and His fury upon all their armies. . . . . And all the host of heaven shall be dissolved, and the heavens shall be rolled together as a scroll: and all their host shall fall down as the leaf falleth off from the vine, and as the falling fig from the fig-tree."[2] Thus does the Lord speak of a time fearful with exceeding terror for all nations of the earth, heralding the advent of the Judge of all.

The words of JEREMIAH's prophecy are no less conclusive than those of Isaiah. Note, for example, the

[1] Isa. xiii. 11–13.   [2] Isa. xxxiv. 1–4.

twenty-fifth chapter, wherein he dwells so strongly upon the judgments of the latter day. "The Lord shall roar from on high, and utter His voice from His holy habitation," when He shall "plead with all flesh," and "give them that are wicked to the sword. Behold, evil shall go forth from nation to nation, and a great whirlwind shall be raised up from the coasts of the earth. And the slain of the Lord shall be, at that day, from one end of the earth even unto the other end of the earth." [1]

The prophet JOEL also foretells important details of the "last days." "Proclaim ye this among the Gentiles; Prepare war, wake up the mighty men, let all the men of war draw near; let them come up; beat your plough-shares into swords, and your pruning-hooks into spears: let the weak say, I am strong. Assemble yourselves, and come, all ye heathen, and gather yourselves together round about: thither cause Thy mighty ones to come down, O Lord. Let the heathen be wakened, and come up to the valley of Jehoshaphat; for there will I sit to judge all the heathen round about. Put ye in the sickle, for the harvest is ripe: come, get you down; for the press is full, the fats overflow; for their wickedness is great. Multitudes, multitudes in the valley of decision." And this shall come to pass as that foretold

[1] Jer. xxv. 32, 33.

time approaches, when "the sun and moon shall be darkened, and the stars shall withdraw their shining," and "the Lord shall roar out of Zion, and utter His voice from Jerusalem; and the heavens shall shake; and the Lord will be the hope of His people, and the strength of the children of Israel;" and men shall know that the Lord dwelleth in Zion; and Jerusalem shall be holy, and there shall no strangers pass through her any more; but Judah shall dwell for ever, and Jerusalem from generation to generation.[1]

And so we might quote from Prophet after Prophet. But we have enough to show us, beyond doubt, that when the Lord shall come again upon this earth it will be in the midst of *great tribulation; the heathen raging; the people imagining a vain thing; the kings of the earth setting themselves together against the Lord and against His Anointed.*[2] There will be, indeed, "a voice of lamentation, and of bitter weeping:" the antitype of Rachel weeping for her children, and refusing to be comforted because they are not:[3] for the wine-press of the wrath of God shall be trodden.

But there shall be OTHER CAUSES OF SAD TROUBLE in the last days, besides those to which we have now referred.

Satan, knowing "that he hath but a short time," will

[1] Joel iii.   [2] Psalm ii. 1, 2.   [3] Jer. xxxi. 15.

grow *desperate*. He will "come down, having great wrath."[1] A peculiar power will be permitted, and he will exercise it wisely. There shall be "fearful sights and great wonders; blood and fire, and pillars of smoke;" "doctrines of devils" advocated and received; "wandering spirits" communicated with, heeded, and trusted;"[2] men energized by Satan, and empowered to work miracles upon the earth—of kind without example on the page of history; iniquity and craft performing such astounding deeds "as to deceive, if it were possible, even the elect;"[3] the earth filled full of "trouble and darkness, dimness and anguish;" so that men in their multitudes shall be "driven to darkness."

Thus wickedness and tribulation, terrible and increasing, shall be found among the characteristics of

---

[1] Rev. xii. 12.

[2] "Now the Spirit speaketh expressly, that in the latter days some shall depart from the faith, giving heed to seducing (πλανοις, *i.e., wandering*) spirits, and doctrines of *devils, speaking lies in hypocrisy*" (1 Tim. iv. 1, 2). See also Isa. viii. 19–22; 2 Thess. ii. 3–12; Rev. xiii. 11–16, and xvi. 13, 14. This subject is very faithfully dealt with in a little work by Rev. E. Nangle, M.A., Rector of Skreen, entitled *Spiritualism Fairly Tried* (Wertheim and Macintosh). The marvellous spread of "Spiritualism," among the upper and middle classes of society, both in England and abroad, should not pass unobserved, though the word of warning to the Lord's people must be "Touch it not." Sixteen years have passed since the first edition of this work was issued, during which time the growth of this baneful evil has been great indeed.   [3] Matt. xxiv. 24.

THE WORLD as the great day of the Lord draws near, and there shall be no such thing as that gradual increase of true enlightenment, righteousness, and peace, which so many persons think will usher in the gentle reign of the Redeemer. For aught then which we learn from the state of things around us in the world, we may be even at the present moment *drawing near* to the great Advent of our God.

But what as to the CHURCH? This is a point of deepest interest with the Lord's people. The world will always be at work for its own master, and therefore it is no marvel if it reap the fruit of such a servitude: but how the children of the Lord will fare amid the increase of wickedness, and in the day of vengeance, is a matter as to which the earnest Christian *must desire* to be informed. The judgments we have spoken of are to be *world-wide*. Exceptions seem to have been made but sparingly on the prophetic page. A man is to be "more precious than the golden wedge of Ophir." "The slain of the Lord" are to be "from one end of the earth to the other." "When the Lord cometh *shall He find faith*" —*shall He find a real Christian*—"upon the earth?" But how is this to be? Will the Lord's people then deny their faith, consort with the wicked, and be consumed with the transgressors? Surely not! The

people of the Lord are many;—multitudes in every
nation under heaven. We cannot think they will apostatize. Nay, who shall make such multitudes afraid?
Moreover, the Inspired Word is plain upon the point.
They shall not apostatize. The iniquity and tribulation
shall be such as to deceive even the Elect "if it were
possible;" but it is *not possible*; as Christ has said,
"My sheep hear My voice and I know them, and they
follow Me, and I give unto them eternal life, *and they
shall never perish, neither shall any (man) pluck them out
of My hand.*" [1] Indeed a great change must pass upon
the world before the day *can* come wherein the Church
of Christ upon the earth, taken as a whole, will be the
subject of a persecution unto death. It is true that both
Daniel [2] and John [3] speak clearly upon the subject of a
last great persecution which is to afflict God's servants;
and *that* immediately before the coming of the Lord for
judgment. But if we examine what they say as to the
state of things which will exist upon the earth at that
period (as we must presently), we shall see that the
whole aspect of the world's affairs will have undergone
a change, sudden and wonderful, brought about by
God Himself.

The strongest intimation which occurs in Scripture

---

[1] John x. 27, 28.   [2] Dan. vii. 25 and xi. 31–37.

[3] Rev. xx. 4.

about the spread of Gospel faith and the spiritual standing of the Church—its zeal, its devotedness, its love for
souls, and its position of power in the world when the
great day is near, appears to be that which our Lord
Jesus Christ Himself gave to His disciples when He
said, "this gospel of the kingdom shall be preached in
all the world, for a witness unto all nations; and then
shall the end come."[1] But this says very little in the
direction of *an universal reception* of the Gospel. The
Gospel is to be *preached* everywhere, "for a witness."
Not to be *received* everywhere, nor even by *every nation*.
Nothing more indeed need be done, nothing more need
be expected than we find to have already taken place.
For anything that is declared in this passage, we may
expect the Second Advent of our Saviour *now*. It is
marvellous how *little* we read in Scripture about the
spiritual standing of the Church of Christ as the
Millennial age approaches, and how *much* we read of
the abounding wickedness of *the world*, its sinfulness
increasing, its evil seducers waxing worse and worse,
deceiving and being deceived.

By what is said respecting the amazing growth of
wickedness in the last days, I think we may expect that
the true people of the Lord will appear more decidedly
distinct, and that they will stand out to greater dis-

[1] Matt. xxiv. 25.

advantage in the eyes of men. Not, however, that mankind will be in the main *without religion.* Very evidently otherwise. *Religiousness* will be a mark of the last days. Men will have "a *form* of godliness, but *deny the power* thereof;" they will be "ever learning, but never able to come to the knowledge of the truth;"[1] preparing themselves, although they know it not, for the worship of that wicked one, whose coming shall be "after the power of Satan," and who "as God," sitting in the Temple of God, will show himself "that he *is* God."[2]

SATISFACTORY, therefore, the state of the professing Church will *not* be. And the *true* Church of the Lord's believing people will be MUCH TRIED. There will be an urgent call for watchfulness and prayer, that the things which remain and are ready to die may be strengthened; there will be need for looking well both to the girdle and the lamp, and for the maintenance of a simple childlike faith in the all-sufficient Saviour.

But here seems to be a *contradiction.* We have seen that the Church will not apostatize—that a persecution unto death (so far as the *whole* Church is concerned) will not take place; and yet that our Lord Himself has intimated, and the Inspired Writers have led us clearly to conclude, that when the Judge of all men shall

[1] 2 Tim. iii. 3-5.   [2] 2 Thess. ii. 4.

descend upon the earth, it will be, as it were, a question whether He will find *one true believer there;* whether there will be any Church whatever in the world to welcome His appearing. In other words—that there *will be* a people ready, waiting, watching for the Lord's Advent, and yet that there will be no faith, no love, no readiness, and no expectancy, but only sin, misery, and anguish of heart, among the multitudes of earth.

But there is *no real contradiction* here; all is plain and clear, although the solution of the difficulty may perchance oppose itself to the ideas prevailing among Christian people. Let us, however, proceed to an examination of this matter.

We will again refer to our Lord's assertion, "As the days of Noe were, so shall the coming of the Son of Man be. . . . As it was in the days of Lot . . . even thus shall it be in the day when the Son of Man is revealed." [1]

NOAH was safely shut within the ark, for "God shut him in" [2] *before* the flood descended upon the earth. And LOT was lodged in the little city ZOAR, which was given as an answer to his prayers, *before* the fire and brimstone were poured down on Sodom. We remember how the destroying angel bade him quickly leave the doomed city: "Haste thee, escape thither (that is, to

---

[1] Luke xvii. 26–30, and elsewhere.   [2] Gen. vii. 17.

Zoar), *for I cannot do anything* till thou be come thither." [1] So THEN IT SHALL BE WHEN THE SON OF MAN IS REVEALED. The waiting people of the Lord *shall be delivered:* they shall be taken to a *place of safety* ere the fearful burden of the last great tribulation shall descend upon the earth's inhabitants.

Further; in the text which forms the heading of this chapter we find our Saviour forewarning His disciples: "Take heed, lest at any time your hearts be overcharged with surfeiting, and drunkenness, and cares of this life, and so that day come upon you *unawares.* For as a snare shall it come ON ALL THEM THAT DWELL ON THE FACE OF THE WHOLE EARTH. Watch ye, therefore, and pray always, that ye may be accounted worthy to *escape* all those things that shall come to pass, and to stand before the Son of Man." Surely this makes matters very plain. The day of Christ shall come "*unawares*" upon "*all* them that dwell on the face of the *whole earth.*" None shall be prepared for it. But it is not thus to come upon the *waiting servants* of the Lord. They will be accounted worthy to escape (ἐκφυγεῖν to flee out of) all those terrors which the people of the world must suffer—the distress of nations, the perplexity, the fear, which shall make men's hearts to fail, and the shaking of the powers of heaven. They shall but "see

---

[1] Gen. xix. 21-23.

these things *begin* to come to pass," and then they shall be called away, and "*stand before the Son of Man.*"[1]

The APOSTLE PAUL, likewise, has a word for us concerning this important matter in his First Epistle to the Thessalonians. It reads as follows: "If we believe that Jesus died and rose again, even so them *also* which sleep in Jesus will God bring with Him."[2] "Them ALSO!" Who then *besides* them shall form a portion of His train? He tells us: "For this we say unto you by the word of the Lord, that we which are alive and remain until the coming of our Lord, shall *not prevent* [that is, "go before" or "be in advance of"] them which are asleep. For the Lord Himself shall descend from Heaven with a shout, with the voice of the Archangel and with the trump of God; and the *dead in Christ shall rise* FIRST. THEN *we which are alive and remain* shall be caught up together with them in the clouds *to meet the Lord in the air.*"[3] Let us observe the order. The *dead* in Christ *first*, and *then* the *living* in Christ are to go and "*meet the Lord in the air*" as He descends from above, that He may "*bring*" them "*with Him*" to the earth among that glorious train which then shall do Him honour. Thus far the testimony of the Apostle Paul is clear. He does not indeed

---

[1] Luke xxi. 34-36. [2] 1 Thes. iv. 14. [3] 1 Thes. iv. 15-17.

tell us what shall take place in the world after the living in Christ shall be changed, and safely taken to the presence of their Lord; but, so far as his testimony goes, it is very decided in support of the doctrine which we have advanced. And if we take his teaching in connexion with that of our Lord, which we have quoted, we shall find it perfectly evident that the Lord's people who shall be living upon the earth at the time of our Saviour's coming, will be caught up to meet Him in the air, and abide with Him in safety till the period of the tribulation shall be over.

Let us now examine what the PROPHETS OF THE OLD TESTAMENT have advanced.

We will turn first to ISAIAH. He has devoted the twenty-fifth and twenty-sixth chapters of his prophecy to the subject now before us. He speaks of a day wherein the Lord will "swallow up death in victory," "wipe away tears from off all faces," and "take away the rebuke of His people from off all the earth;" a day wherein it shall be said, "Lo! this is our God: we have waited for Him, and He will save us;" a day wherein the Lord "will keep him in perfect peace whose mind is stayed on Him;" a day wherein the Lord's hand shall be lifted up, and though the wicked "will not see, they shall see." Now we find a strange word spoken by the prophet concerning these wicked ones who "will not see," and the people who have waited for the Lord. Of the wicked He declares, "They are dead, they *shall not live*: they are deceased, they *shall not rise*: therefore, Thou hast visited and destroyed them, and made all their memory to perish."[1] And then, after an expression of wonder and gratitude to God for the increase and prosperity of Israel, which shall take place at that time, he continues (still addressing God), "*Thy* dead *shall* live, together with my dead body shall they arise." And then (as it were) turning to *the people of the Lord who shall be lying in the silent tomb*, he adds—"Awake and sing, ye that dwell in the dust: for thy dew is as the dew of herbs, and the earth shall cast out the dead." And then again, addressing *others*, he says—"Come, my people, enter thou into thy chambers, and shut thy doors about thee: hide thyself, as it were, for a little moment, until the indignation be overpast. For, behold, the Lord cometh out of His place to punish the inhabitants of the earth for their iniquity: The earth also shall disclose her blood, and shall no more cover her slain." This last address could not certainly have been intended *for the dead*. They—already secure against the sword—would be beyond the reach of comfort from such exhortation: a punishment designed for "the

[1] Isa. xxvi. 14.

inhabitants of the earth" a punishment concerning the effect of which it is declared, "the earth shall disclose her blood, and shall no more cover her slain" —could not be profitable for men *already dead*. The living surely must be addressed here. The living people of the Lord. Those "who are living and remain" unto His coming. Such (speaking after the manner of men) would be unsafe amid the fearful tribulation to be poured out upon the unbelieving world. Therefore, they are *called away before* "the Lord cometh out of His place to punish the inhabitants of the earth for their iniquity."

Let us take the word of another prophet—DANIEL. The twelfth chapter opens thus—"And at that time shall Michael stand up, the great prince which standeth for the children of Thy people; and there shall be a time of trouble, such as never was since there was a nation, even to that same time: and *at that time thy people shall be delivered, every one that shall be found written in the book*. And *many* of them that sleep in the dust of the earth shall awake, some to everlasting life, and some to shame and everlasting contempt."[1] Now, this passage requires a little explanation. It appears that at the time when the great prince shall stand up, there shall be AN UNPRECEDENTED TRIBULATION, but every one whose name "shall be found written in the book"

[1] Dan. xii. 1, 2.

shall be delivered: he shall not be a sufferer: he shall (as we have seen elsewhere) arise to meet the Lord, and abide with Him in safety. Moreover, "*many* of them that sleep in the dust of the earth shall awake." "*Many*"—NOT ALL—*a part only* of the dead. But *who* of these? The passage tells us, as it continues, "Some to everlasting life, and some to shame and everlasting contempt." Here we must remove a *difficulty*. I believe there is an acknowledged incorrectness in rendering the Hebrew words which are translated "some." They should be rendered "these" and "those."[1] With this alteration the passage will read thus, "Many of them that sleep in the dust of the earth shall awake, *these* (who awake) to *everlasting life*, and *those* (who still sleep on in death, are reserved) *to shame and everlasting contempt.*

In Daniel's prophecy, therefore, we find the same important doctrine. The *living saints* shall be changed, and delivered from the tribulation; the *departed saints* shall be raised, and enter into everlasting life. The *wicked among the living* shall be left to go through the time of trouble; the *wicked among the departed* shall be

---

[1] וְאֵלֶּה . . . . אֵלֶּה in Hebrew are the same as *hi et illi*, in Latin, viz., "these and these, or these and those;" as indeed we find the same words translated in Isaiah xlix. 12, "Behold *these* shall come from afar, and *these* from the coast of Sinim."

reserved for a *future* resurrection day, when they shall arise "to shame and everlasting contempt."

That we may yet more fully establish the fact before us, let us turn attention for a moment to an allegory which occurs in the twelfth chapter of the Book of Revelation, where the approach of the end of this dispensation is referred to under the vision of "the seventh trumpet." The Church of Christ is brought before us under the figure of A WOMAN CLOTHED WITH THE SUN, whose *child*, about to be born, is anxiously waited for by *the Dragon :* but as soon as he is brought forth, *God interferes on his behalf, and he is caught up to heaven.* This done, the persecution commences against the woman, and continues for a thousand two hundred and threescore days. This persecution is accompanied by a word of woe to the inhabitants of the earth and of the sea, for that the devil is come down to them, having great wrath, because he knoweth that he hath but a short time. This allegory speaks for itself. I assume that the woman represents the entire Church of God, pertaining to all ages. There is no room, I think, for doubt that this is the meaning; indeed the position of the allegory proves it. But if this be granted, the details scarcely need a word of explanation. The Church, *immediately before the Great Tribulation*, gives forth this, her man-child, to the hand of God, who straightway takes it to Himself.

All, then, is clear so far; and we may conclude, with a very near approach to certainty, that when the day of trouble is about to dawn upon the world, *every one* among God's waiting people—*every sincere believer in the Lord Jesus,* be he living on the earth or buried in the grave— shall rise to meet that great Redeemer in the air, and shall be safe with Him above, until the time arrive when He, with all His saints, shall come to execute His fearful judgments on the earth's inhabitants.

Here let us pause a moment to reflect about *ourselves.* If the trumpet of the Lord should sound this day for the departure of the saints of Christ, *should we be ready ?* It is written, " In that *day,* two men shall be in the field," and again, " in that *night* two men shall be in one bed (for the call will reach to every place upon the surface of our globe, where it is *day,* and where it is *night*), one shall be taken and the other left: two women shall be grinding together, one shall be taken and the other left." [1]   Which then would it be in our case ?   TAKEN OR LEFT ?   If we are putting off the things of our eternity to a future day, we should be LEFT.   If we have not gone as helpless sinners to the Lord Jesus Christ, that we might obtain pardon through His blood, we should be LEFT.   But if we have, through grace, with all our hearts sought the Redeemer, laid our

[1] Matt. xxiv. 40, 41 ; Luke xvii. 34, 36.

sins on Him by faith, received Him as our Lord and
Saviour in sincerity and truth, then we should be TAKEN
—taken up to meet our King, and be with Him for ever.
Let us see—each one for himself—that we are not found
wanting in the sight of the Great Judge of all.

But further. We must inquire as to the state of
things upon the earth when the people of the Lord shall
have been called away. The woman in the apocalyptic
allegory fled into the wilderness, and remained there for
three years and a half, nourished and protected by God,
after her man-child had been caught up. There shall be,
therefore, I assume, even while the tribulation lasts,
A TRUE AND FAITHFUL CHURCH: persecuted, but not
forsaken; for we read that "the serpent cast out of his
mouth water as a flood, that he might cause the woman
to be carried away thereby;" and that "the dragon was
wroth with the woman, and went to make war with the
remnant of her seed which keep the commandments of
God, and have the testimony of Jesus Christ." This
allegorical evidence of a Church existing and persecuted,
after the first-fruits have been removed, is corroborated by
another passage, more clear and free from allegory, in
the twentieth chapter. Here we find the Apostle John,
when speaking of the introduction of the millennial
reign, making reference to certain persons who should
suffer martyrdom under "*the Beast*" (which is—as we

shall show hereafter—the name given to the future Antichrist in the Book of Revelation); martyrs, therefore who are to suffer death *after the first-fruits of the earth shall have departed.* His word is as follows: "I saw thrones, and they sat upon them, and judgment was given unto them. And I saw the souls of them that were beheaded for the witness of Jesus and for the Word of God, and *which had not worshipped the Beast,* neither his image, neither had received his mark in their foreheads or in their hands; and they lived and reigned with Christ a thousand years."

Thus it is evident that *after* the departure of the first-fruits, *after* the man-child shall be caught up to heaven, *after* the Lord's waiting people shall be taken away to meet their Saviour in the air, there shall be found a CHURCH—a people serving Christ in truth; and against these a persecution shall be effectually directed, even unto death.

But a great difficulty arises here. *Every believer will have gone. A vast multitude out of every nation under heaven will have been taken hence.* The Lord will have descended into the heights above the world; *invisibly, perhaps, to all except His people*—I say INVISIBLY TO ALL EXCEPT HIS PEOPLE, for I think there is no warrant given us in Holy Scripture for asserting that there shall be *any token* granted to the unconverted world *before the tribulation*, to warn them of the descent of Jesus into the air to call His saints. The unbelievers may not, perhaps, be startled by the trumpet-sound, nor even see a lightning flash. They will, indeed, be witnesses of these things "*immediately after* the tribulation of those days," as the twenty-fourth chapter of Matthew testifies, but. *this shall be* "*after* the tribulation of those days." Probably the dead in Christ will be raised without exciting the suspicion of mankind that an event so wonderful is taking place. No stone displaced ; no sod upturned ; no grave disturbed ; only the body gone. Then, as suddenly, the removal of the *living* people of the Lord will follow. In *silence* also, and *without a sign* afforded to the unbelieving world (for anything that has appeared in Scripture to the contrary). They will be taken hence —drawn up at once to Christ. They will be missed and sought for upon earth, but nowhere found. In every neighbourhood will be the cry for them. In house after house will be a bitter wailing because of them. Oh, what a day of sadness and terror that will be ! What dread will sit on every countenance ! For thus shall the world be in one moment stripped of all the pure, and just, and holy who adorned its surface, and be left a WICKED WORLD INDEED.

But what may we expect will *follow*, if the day of grace be not for ever at that moment closed? Most

certainly A GREAT REVIVAL OF RELIGION. For imagine
the sensation which must be produced among the unconverted masses by the sudden removal of each Christian
from the surface of the whole earth. *One, two, three,*
out of every family *gone,* no man can tell where—passed
from sight in the twinkling of an eye! Two in a bed—
one taken ! two at a mill—*one taken !* two friends con-
versing—*one taken !* two men transacting business—*one
taken !* Husband and wife, brother and sister, master
and servant—*one taken !* Will not men begin to think?
Will not many scoffers fall upon their knees and pray?
Will not the Bible be searched with new eyes? Will
not men's hearts fail them for fear, and for looking after
those things which are coming upon the earth? Oh!
methinks there will be a stirring up of lukewarm
ministers in that day—a crowding into churches such as
never has been witnessed. A *change, indeed,* will come
over the face of the earth's society. And so indeed we
find it stated—when this matter is dealt with in the
fourteenth chapter of the Revelation—that *immediately*
the first-fruits unto God and the Lamb are spoken of as
being with the Lord above, *an angel* flies through the
midst of heaven, " having the everlasting Gospel to
preach to them that dwell on the earth, and to every
nation, and kindred, and tongue, and people; saying
with a loud voice, Fear God, and give glory to Him, for

the hour of His judgment is come."[1] But clearly,
though there may be many who will truly turn to God
in that day, yet the devil will find means to blind the
masses of the world to the true state of things; for, as
we pursue the chapter, we perceive that after Babylon
is fallen, which is the next event that will transpire,
and Antichrist is established upon his throne, "*the
patience of the saints*" is brought before us; and it is
added, "Blessed are the dead which die in the Lord
from henceforth."[2] And immediately takes place the
HARVEST OF THE EARTH, which seems to be a second
gathering together of God's people unto Him—partly
through the medium of a fearful burst of persecution,
which shall clear the earth of multitudes who shall
refuse the mark and worship of the Beast—and partly
by the arm of His deliverance saving such as called
upon His Name—and so the number of the Lord's elect
will be complete, and the way be rendered clear for the
tremendous VINTAGE OF THE WRATH OF GOD.[3]

So far, then,—guided by the simple word of Holy
Scripture,—have we been able to obtain some most
important intimations of THE STATE IN WHICH THE
WORLD AND THE CHURCH WILL BE FOUND when the
Advent of the Lord draws near.

I ask you not to take these things for granted, either

[1] Rev. xiv. 6, 7.   [2] Rev. xiv. 13.   [3] Rev. xiv. 20.

that they *are* or *are not* as I have placed them now before you. But I beg of you, as those *deeply interested* in such momentous matters, which must—sooner or later—come upon the earth, to search the Bible *without prejudice,* and without reference to *preconceived ideas,* and see for yourselves accurately how these matters stand. And then, as you value your immortal souls, look well to your own state with God. Are you in Christ? Are you forgiven? Are you saved? Oh! what is your condition *now* before the King of kings? I would urge upon you, *settle these important questions.* See that you are Christ's indeed, that you *believe in Him,* and are *alive* through His atoning blood and justifying righteousness—alive to God—the children of His grace and love. Then if speedily the summons should go forth from the high throne of Heaven, "COME UP HITHER!" you will obey with joy, leave earthly things as dross uncared for more, and depart hence arrayed in glory, meet for those who sit with the eternal King upon the Throne of His dominion.

CHAPTER III.

Israel and Antichrist.

"If another shall come in his own name, him ye will receive."
JOHN v. 43.

HAVING shown, I hope distinctly, that as the day of Christ approaches, the World will display growth in wickedness, and the Church will be caught up to be for ever with the Lord, the question will be asked—"What is to be the state OF THAT PECULIAR PEOPLE WITH WHOM, AS A NATION, GOD HAS ENTERED INTO SO REMARKABLE A COVENANT?"

To the NATION OF ISRAEL and to that ANTICHRIST with whom that nation in the latter days will have a marvellous connection, I shall devote this chapter.

Four thousand years have nearly passed away since the Almighty said to Abraham, "I will make of thee a great nation . . . and in thee shall all the families of the earth be blessed." [1] Not long after this preliminary

[1] Gen. xii. 1–3.

promise had been made, the patriarch was called upon to lift his eyes, and look from the place where he was standing, northward, southward, eastward, and westward; and God said unto him—" All the land which thou seest, to thee will I give it, and to thy seed for ever." [1]   And, on another occasion, very expressly,— " Unto thy seed have I given this land, from the river of Egypt unto the great river, the river Euphrates." [2] This promise is laid down still *more* clearly in the BOOK OF EXODUS, where God declared to Israel, " I will set thy bounds from the *Red Sea* even unto the *Sea of the Philistines*, and from the *Desert* unto the *River*." [3]   And so again, in DEUTERONOMY, " Every place whereon the soles of your feet shall tread shall be yours, from the *Wilderness and Lebanon*, from the River, *the River Euphrates*, even unto the *Uttermost Sea* shall your coast be." [4]   The extent of this promise seems to me to cover THE WHOLE VAST PENINSULA OF ARABIA.[5]   Indeed, I think, a careful perusal of the limits of the land of

---

[1] Gen. xiii. 14, 15.   [2] Gen. xv. 18.

[3] Exod. xxiii. 31.   [4] Deut. xi. 24.

[5] Rule a line from the northern point of the district of *Lebanon* to the southern point of that of *Sinai*, and draw a perpendicular to it. You will then find that the SEA of OMAN is "*the Uttermost Sea.*" And again, start from the River Euphrates, and draw a perpendicular from the average line of its course, and the RED SEA is "*the Uttermost Sea.*" Thus the whole peninsula of Arabia will be included. (See *Interpretations of Prophecy*, by Major Scott Phillips.)

Israel (*as they shall be*) which are given in the forty-seventh chapter of EZEKIEL will show, with clearness, that this will be the true extent of Israel's territory. But be it as it may; the promises of God to Israel in their obvious meaning have reference to an *actual* and *perpetual possession* of the land. Now the time has *not yet been* when the children of Israel enjoyed an *actual possession* even from the Euphrates to the Mediterranean; except, perhaps, for a brief period during the days of Solomon, of whom it is said, "he reigned over all the kings from the river even unto the land of the Philistines and to the border of Egypt;"[1] but even in that prosperous day we do not read that Israel enjoyed such *absolute possession* as the promises would lead us to expect. Moreover, the strongest and most enlarged predictions as to Israel's inheritance have reference to a period which shall have its dawn when the twelve tribes, dispersed among the nations, shall have been gathered, and "the times of the Gentiles" "fulfilled." This period is yet to come.

We will establish this position by reference to a few passages from the PROPHETS, passages which certainly forbid — if any language can forbid — a construction which is not *strictly literal*. Hear now first what is written by ISAIAH: "It shall come to pass in that day,

[1] 2 Chron. ix. 26.

that the Lord shall set His hand again *the second time* to recover the remnant of His people, which shall be left, from Assyria, and from Egypt, and from Pathros, and from Cush, and from Elam, and from Shinar, and from Hamath, and from the Islands of the Sea. And He shall set up an ensign for the nations, and *shall assemble the outcasts of Israel, and gather the dispersed of Judah from the four corners of the earth.*"[1] But what is *that day* which is here referred to as the period when this *second recovery* shall take place? Certainly it is *not* a day which has yet dawned upon the sons of men, for in *that* day, the Prophet says, "The wolf shall dwell with the lamb; and the leopard shall lie down with the kid; and the calf and the young lion and the fatling together; and a little child shall lead them. . . . . And the earth shall be full of the knowledge of the Lord, as the waters cover the sea."

Observe JEREMIAH's language: "Hear the word of the Lord, O ye nations, and declare it in the isles afar off, and say, He that scattered Israel *will gather him* and keep him as a shepherd doth his flock; for the Lord hath redeemed Jacob, and ransomed him from the hand of him that was stronger than he. *Therefore, they shall come and sing in the heights of Zion, and shall flow together to the goodness of the Lord,* for wheat, and

---

[1] Isaiah xi. ; see also ch. xviii., xxxiii., and li.

for wine, and for oil, and for the young of the flock and of the herd: and their soul shall be as a watered garden, and *they shall not sorrow any more at all.*"[1] Surely Israel has never thus been gathered hitherto. Her tribes still sorrow as they have been wont for many centuries. This gathering, therefore, must be *future*.

Refer, also, to Ezekiel. From the thirty-sixth chapter to the end of the prophecy, we find *this subject only* brought before us. It occupies thirteen chapters. In the course of these we cannot fail to note the unmistakable language which the Lord uses—"*I will take you from among the heathen, and gather you out of all countries, and will bring you unto your own land.* Then will I sprinkle clean water upon you, and ye shall be clean. . . . . A new heart also will I give you, and ye *shall dwell in the land that I gave to your fathers;* and ye shall be My people, and I will be your God.*"[2] . . . . "Behold, O My people, I will open your graves, and cause you to come up out of your graves, and *bring you into the land of Israel.*[3] Behold I will *take the children of Israel from among the heathen, whither they be gone, and will gather them on every side, and bring them into their own land.* And I will make them *one nation* in the land upon the mountains of Israel; and one king

[1] Jer. xxxi. 10–12, 37–40 ; xxxiii. 7–26.
[2] Ezek. xxxvi. 24–28.   [3] Ezek. xxxvii. 12-14.

shall be king to them all; and they shall be *no more two nations,* neither shall they be divided into two kingdoms any more at all. . . . . Moreover, I will make a covenant of peace with them; it shall be an everlasting covenant with them; and I will place them, and multiply them, and will set My sanctuary in the midst of them for evermore." [1]

Surely these predictions have not yet received accomplishment. But the WORD OF GOD IS TRUE, and Israel's day for restoration WILL arrive.

We might refer to other passages in EZEKIEL, or quote from HOSEA,[2] JOEL,[3] AMOS,[4] MICAH,[5] ZEPHANIAH,[6] ZECHARIAH, or MALACHI. The last two mentioned prophesied *after the return from Babylon,* wherefore their testimony is peculiarly conclusive. Let us dwell for an instant on their words.

ZECHARIAH says, "I will strengthen the house of Judah and I will save the house of Joseph, and I will *bring them again to place them,* for I will have mercy upon them, and *they shall be as though I had not cast them off.* . . . . They shall remember Me in far countries, and they shall live with their children, and *turn again.* I will *bring them again also out of the land of Egypt, and*

---

[1] Ezek. xxxvii. 21–28.
[2] Hosea iii. 4, 5.
[3] Joel iii. 16, 17.
[4] Amos ix. 11–15.
[5] Micah iii. 12 ; iv. 1, 2.
[6] Zeph. iii. 14–20.

*gather them out of Assyria, and I will bring them again
into the land of Gilead and Lebanon."* [1] "In that day
will I make the Governors of Judah like an hearth of
fire among the wood.....And Jerusalem shall be
inhabited again in her own place, even in Jerusalem. The
Lord also shall save the tents of *Judah first.....* In
that day there shall be a fountain opened to the house
of David, and to the inhabitants of Jerusalem, for sin,
and for uncleanness.....And men shall dwell in it
(Jerusalem), and there shall be *no more utter destruction;
but Jerusalem shall be safely inhabited.* In that day
shall there be upon the bells of the horses HOLINESS
UNTO THE LORD.....Yea, every pot in Jerusalem and
in Judah shall be holiness unto the Lord of Hosts." [2]
What language can be plainer? Where can room be
found for a mere spiritual interpretation?

From MALACHI, the last of the prophets, we take our
final passage — written one hundred years after the
return from Babylon: "I will rebuke the devourer for
your sakes..... *All nations shall call you blessed; for
ye shall be a delightsome land,* saith the Lord of Hosts." [3]

As to the NEW TESTAMENT witness we need not speak
at length. Few passages therein have reference to
Israel's restoration; still quite enough is said to show

---

[1] Zech. x. 6, 7.   [2] Zech. xii. 6, 7 ; xiii., xiv.
[3] Mal. iii. 11, 12.

that the abundant testimony of the prophets must be *recognised.*

OUR LORD declares, " Jerusalem shall be trodden down of the Gentiles, *until the times of the Gentiles be fulfilled;* "[1] which clearly implies that Jerusalem shall be, *after that, no longer trodden down.* Concerning CHRIST it is declared, " The Lord God shall give unto Him the *throne of His father David, and He shall reign over the house of Jacob for ever,* and of His kingdom there shall be *no end.*"[2] But how is this to be, except a restoration of Israel shall take place? Again, the first sermon preached by an Apostle testifies that David, "being a prophet," knew "that God had sworn with an oath to him, that of the fruit of his loins, *according to the flesh,* he would raise up Christ *to sit on his throne.*"[3] And in the second apostolic sermon we read thus, "Repent ye therefore, and be converted, that your sins may be blotted out, when *the times of refreshing* shall come from the presence of the Lord, and *He shall send Jesus Christ,* which before was preached unto you; whom the heavens must receive *until the restitution of all things,* which God hath spoken by the mouth of all His holy prophets since the world began."[4] Then there *shall* be a "time of refreshing" and "RESTITUTION OF

---

[1] Luke xxi. 24. [2] Luke i. 33.
[3] Acts ii. 30. [4] Acts iii. 19–21.

F

ALL THINGS" when the Lord Jesus Christ shall come from heaven; and, having come, shall sit upon the throne of David. Thus did the Apostle PETER testify. PAUL also, in no less than three chapters[1] of his Epistle to the Romans, dwells upon the Lord's dealings with Israel and the Gentiles, and shows clearly that the many prophecies which went before upon this point *have not received accomplishment.* "Hath God cast away His people?" he asks. "God forbid" is the reply... .. "I would not, brethren, that ye should be ignorant of this mystery, . . . that blindness in part has happened to Israel, *until the fulness of the Gentiles be come in.* And so *all Israel* shall be saved. As it is written, There shall come out of Zion the Deliverer, and shall turn away ungodliness from Jacob: for this is My covenant unto them when I shall take away their sins."[2]

We find evidence enough, then, both in the Old Testament and the New, to prove clearly THAT A DAY OF RESTORATION IS IN STORE FOR ISRAEL; THAT HER TRIBES WILL BE GATHERED AND BROUGHT TO THEIR OWN LAND, and there be placed in a position of greater blessedness than they have ever yet enjoyed.

Let us now inquire further respecting Israel, seeing they have been so long time scattered over all the earth, WHAT THEIR POSITION IS AT PRESENT; whether there

---

[1] Rom. ix., x., xi.   [2] See also Gal. iii.; Heb xii.; and Rev. vii.

are *any signs of their return to Palestine;* and generally *how the Lord is dealing with them.*

As of old time, so we see them *still*—without a country, without a city, without a temple, without a king, dispersed among the nations, yet *distinct from all.* In Europe, Asia, Africa, and America, the Jew is to be found; a marked man; important, yet despised; honourable, yet a by-word and reproach. The Israelitish people dwell *alone* though they are *everywhere.* They are not reckoned among the nations.[1] "The precious sons of Zion, comparable to fine gold, how are they esteemed as earthen pitchers, the work of the hands of the potter!"[2] In some respects, however, a great change has come over the whole Jewish people. There are signs of life, of nobility, of an effort on behalf of their nationality, which for the past eighteen hundred years has not existed. Though still distinct as ever from the rest of men—the Lord is leading them from their degraded state to *fill the highest posts of public confidence.* [1]"The number of civic functionaries in FRANCE belonging to the Jewish communion is *immensely larger* than the proportionate Israelitish population. M. Achille Fould, at Paris, is but the head of a cohort of Jewish notabilities, financiers, and employés,

---

[1] Num. xxiii. 9.   [2] Lam. iv. 2.
[1] N.B.—Extract from the *Prophetical Journal* of October, 1862.

who are quite as numerous in the departments as in the capital. At Lyons, Marseilles, and other towns of the South, a large number of the higher government officials are Jews; and at Epinal, the chief city of the department of the Vosges, there is the curious spectacle of the four most eminent civic functionaries—the paymaster, the military superintendent, the president of the court of justice, and the keeper-general of forests, being *Jews, one and all.* Scarcely a century ago, the Jews were hunted like mad dogs in the dominion of the Kaiser, at the mercy of every monk or police officer, and without the slightest security for life and property. Now, in this year, 1862, *two eloquent Jews are the leaders of the great liberal party of the Austrian Reichsrath, and Emperor and Imperial Ministers tremble before the names of Giskra and Kuranda.* More marked than even in Austria is the rise of the Jews in PRUSSIA. In the present political agitation, *Hebrew leaders* play the most conspicuous part, and their participation in the recent elections was so pronounced that the *Kreux Zeitung* for weeks did scarcely anything else but abuse the so-styled Jew democrats. According to this paper, nearly one-fourth the number of *Wäller* chosen by the people of Prussia to elect the deputies was composed of Jews—a number about *twenty times as large as is warranted by the population of the kingdom.* At Berlin and other

large towns the Hebrew preponderance was still more
conspicuous ; and in some of the ancient Polish provinces
the descendants of Abraham had it all their own way. On
classifying the students of the universities and high
schools, the startling result is displayed that the superior
academies are attended by *five times as many Jews in
proportion to Christians,* regard, of course, being had to
the general population, of which the Israelites form
scarcely one and a-half per cent. The educated Jews
form part in all the revolutionary movements from the
Ural to the Atlantic, and from Lapland to Sicily.
They are, as it were, the yeast of the European fer-
mentation. The Jew element is perceptible in the
Galician peasantry, in the Finnish malcontents, in the
Servian progressists, and in the surging masses of revolutionary Poland."[1]   Moreover, it is confidently
stated that wheresoever *of late* the Jew is found—
whether in Scandinavia, in Continental Europe, in
England, on the edge of the North African sea-shore,
or in the desert of the South—he has lost the
downcast hopelessness of former years ; a change has
come over him ; he feels his membership with a nation

[1] N.B.—The first Edition of this work was published in 1863. Hence
this quotation from a periodical bearing date 1862.   I retain it in
this Edition because since that time the progress of the Jews has been
steadily advancing, and their position has become yet more honourable
in every nation.

which is rising into greatness; his face is looking towards Jerusalem, and he expects with confidence that the day is close at hand when he shall return to the land of the covenant, and inherit the fruition of the promises.

Besides this, *all is getting ready for the reception of Israel in the* HOLY LAND. There is wealth there. Cultivation is going on, and fruitfulness follows. JERUSALEM itself has undergone a change. The city, not many years ago, was poor and miserable in its appearance, the houses mean and dirty, the streets narrow and crooked. *Now* the streets are wide and straight, and alive with the busy hum of traffic. Many handsome buildings have been erected, with beautiful gardens attached, in which flourish all the luscious fruits of this favoured clime. Fine churches, synagogues, hospitals, dispensaries, hotels, and stores are everywhere met with; and rich men from Constantinople, Babylon, Bagdad, Damascus, Egypt, England, France, and other places, have contributed by their presence to improve and beautify Jerusalem.[1] Preparation, then, is going on in Israel's ancient capital; and seeing it is evident that the heart of all the nation is set earnestly upon the hallowed territory, and that the people are obtaining power in the world, and favour also, of no ordinary kind; I know not what now hinders but that we may

---

[1] Taunton's *Days in which we Live.*

seriously expect the sons of Israel will speedily call Palestine their own, and people that long-promised land with those WHOSE RIGHT IT IS.

A most important question here comes before us, viz. : IN WHAT STATE AS TO RELIGION will the tribes of Israel be when they return to Palestine? Will they *first embrace the Gospel?* or will they be restored *in unbelief?*

We find the LORD thus speaking by Ezekiel : "Because ye are all become dross; behold, I will gather you in the midst of Jerusalem. As they gather silver, and brass, and iron, and lead, and tin, into the midst of the furnace to blow the fire upon it, to melt it, so will I gather you *in mine anger and in my fury, and I will* LEAVE YOU THERE AND MELT YOU. Yea, I will gather you, and blow upon you in the fire of my wrath, and ye shall be melted in the midst thereof : as silver is melted in the midst of the furnace, so shall ye be melted in the midst thereof : and ye shall know that I THE LORD *have poured out My fury upon you.*" Now this gathering of Israel was to be *after* they should have been scattered among the heathen, and dispersed in the countries, and *after* they should have been so dealt with that the heart of the nation, could not " endure," nor the hands thereof be " strong."[1] This language is not certainly consistent with the return of Israel in a *converted* state ; neither,

[1] Ezek. xxii.

indeed, is that of any other part of Scripture. But rather the whole voice of prophecy bids us *first* behold the tribes of Israel (or *part thereof*) gathered and established in the land of their fathers, and then *afterwards*, the Spirit of the Lord outpoured upon their sin-bound hearts. But I will not dwell further upon this interesting question at the present point, because it will necessarily come before us again as we proceed.

Another subject for inquiry of no slight importance comes before us with regard to Israel's return. WHO SHALL BE THEIR LEADER? UNDER WHOSE AUSPICES WILL THEIR RETURN TO PALESTINE BE BROUGHT ABOUT? BY WHOM WILL THE LAND OF THE COVENANT BE PLACED IN THEIR POSSESSION? WHAT POTENTATE WILL IN- TEREST HIMSELF IN THEIR RESTORATION, AND TAKE THEIR CASE IN HAND?

We answer—so far as Judah, Benjamin, and Levi are concerned—ANTICHRIST. The ANTICHRIST will restore the Jews!!! The GREAT OPPONENT of the God of Israel will fulfil the Lord's most Holy Word, and carry out His hallowed purposes. To suit his own ungodly ends he will make a league with the peculiar people, adhere thereto for a short time, then *break* it, and be the instrument of bringing about a tribulation, in which the Jews shall be sufferers indeed—a tribu- lation such as has not been since the world was.

For awhile we will give attention to this ANTICHRIST. Afterwards the case of Israel will come again before our notice.

In the twelfth chapter of REVELATION, upon which we have already dwelt, we read of "WAR IN HEAVEN"[1] —"And there was War in Heaven; Michael and his angels fought against the Dragon, and the Dragon fought and his angels, and prevailed not; neither was their place found any more in Heaven. And the great Dragon was cast out, that old serpent, called the Devil and Satan, which deceiveth the whole world; he was cast out into the Earth, and his angels were cast out with him." This prophecy concerning "War in Heaven" is introduced indeed in the midst of an *allegory*, and may in a certain measure be *itself allegorical.* Most likely it is so. But *this* is clear; Satan, the devil which deceives the world, is declared to contend some point of serious import, in which the interests of mankind have intimate concern, the angels of God being his opponents. He is overcome, and cast down upon the earth, and may no longer interfere *except upon its surface.* Whether the contest will be (as it were) army against army—spiritual beings in array against spiritual beings; or whether it will be, so to speak, the *moral* force of

[1] See further particulars in notes to *The Book of Revelation in Diagram.* Article "Satan."

Heaven against the *immoral* force of Hell; we cannot
know.   But a contest—a war—*there will be* in some
form or other, and Satan will thenceforth be cast down
and confined to earth, until the day shall come for his
more trying bondage in the pit prepared for his millennial imprisonment.   It would appear from many
parts of Scripture, that the great Arch-Adversary carries
on his work among the sons of men *in our day*, chiefly
through the agency of *his unholy Angels*,[1] "the power
of the air" having liberty to abide "in high (or
heavenly) places," he being their acknowledged "Prince."
But in *the day of the Lord's descent*, the Church with its
great Head will occupy these heights, and Satan will be
cast from their dominion, and descending thence, deprived of all authority, be forced to make *this world his
seat.*   Here, then, among mankind, will all his hellish
force be concentrated: but although thus limited, THE
EVIL ONE WILL NOT BE IDLE.   He will have *great wrath*
knowing that he hath but a short time.[2]

What this conquered, but still wrathful, one will do,
we have now to discover.

I venture an *assertion* before proof.   He will, in
the first place REVEAL THE ANTICHRIST; and then USE
HIM AS A MIGHTY INSTRUMENT FOR RAISING UP A
FEARFUL POWER OF EVIL.   He will reveal the Anti-

---

[1] Eph. vi. 12.   [2] Rev. xii. 12.

christ; that is, he will *take possession of and energize
a man, communicating to him all he can bestow on our
mortality of fiendish power and craft.*

"Ye have heard," said the apostle John, "that
Antichrist (The Antichrist Ὁ Ἀντιχριστος) shall come;
even now there are many Antichrists:" but this shall
be The Antichrist. This is a full title; it means,
the contrary of Christ. The one set over against
Christ, as it were in *mimic correspondence*, bearing out
the peculiar details of Christ's position and offices in
such a manner as to deceive and overthrow the faith
of men. So at least the teaching of the Bible leads us
to expound the word. For we find there, that—as
Christ was a *man in-dwelt by* the Eternal God, so
Antichrist will be a *man in-dwelt by* Satan; as Christ
is the *Second Person in the Trinity of Heaven* (the
Father, the Son, and the Holy Ghost), so Antichrist
will be the *second person in the Trinity of Hell* (the
Devil, the Beast, and the False Prophet); as the *Father
gave not His Spirit by measure unto Christ,* so will not
Satan give his spirit by measure unto Antichrist. Thus
a Man—the contrary of Christ—shall practise and
prosper in the world.

But so astounding and terrible an assertion must not
go unproved. What, then, saith the Scripture?

In the second chapter of the Second Epistle to the

THESSALONIANS, the Apostle tells us of a certain "MAN OF SIN," who must be revealed before "the day of Christ" shall come, and whom he calls "THE SON OF PERDITION." He speaks of him as one "who opposeth, and exalteth himself above all that is called God, or that is worshipped; so that he, as God, sitteth in the Temple of God, showing himself that he is God." Now we cannot fail to observe, that this proud opposer must be a man *yet to be revealed;* for since St. Paul's day there has been *no Temple of God,* wherein such an one should sit. The Temple at Jerusalem *is not:* and no other temple has succeeded it, to which we have received a sanction to apply so honoured a distinction. ST. PETER's at ROME most certainly can lay no claim to such a title with the feeblest ray of justice. Nor can we point to any church or other building in the world which might be singled out amongst its fellows as meriting the name. The Temple of God, therefore, which is spoken of by Paul, must be a temple *yet to be erected,* unless indeed the Church of Christ be intended. But this cannot be, because that Church—the body of the Lord—is the Temple of the Holy Ghost. Wherefore Satan and the man he will energize cannot dwell in that. The only temple of which we *read in Scripture* as a temple for God's worship *to be reared again,* is that of which the full particulars are given by the Prophet

EZEKIEL.[1] But evidently no Man of Sin will sit therein. That will be the Temple of God pertaining to Jerusalem which will adorn Judea in the happy age of the Millennium, when righteousness and peace will reign triumphantly beneath the sway of our Emmanuel's sceptre. But when Israel are restored to their own land, we cannot doubt that their first act will be to build their House for Worship. Their occupation of the Covenant-land would be *as nothing*, if their Temple, their ritual, and their sacrifices, were not present. Now, if, upon the old foundations, the Children of the Covenant should rear the Temple and restore the old Mosaic ritual—if *there*, the God of Abraham (although not acceptably, because without the faith of Jesus) should be praised; if the Word of God (although in part only) should be the word directing all the services and ceremonies, what could that temple be with justice called except the "TEMPLE OF GOD?" Nay, we remember how that even when the ancient Temple, reared by the wicked Herod on the old foundation laid by Zerubbabel, was defiled by usury and hypocrisy, the Lord declared it was "HIS FATHER'S HOUSE." [2] And when the Lord was crucified, and had been preached to, and rejected by, the Jews, the Apostles (being Jews themselves) did not cast off their reverence for the Temple worship. To the

---

[1] Ezek. xl.–xlviii.   [2] John ii. 16.

Temple went up Peter and John at the appointed hour of prayer.[1] There was Paul found in obedience to the Law:[2] and thither he repaired from time to time "to worship" God.[3] To the Apostles (though the Temple service did not recognise the Saviour Jesus as the Son of the Most High) the Temple was no less THE TEMPLE OF THEIR GOD AND FATHER. Indeed how *could* it have been otherwise? And how can any future building standing in its place, erected after the pattern shown to Moses in the Mount, erected *by Israel* for the service of the *God of Israel, be otherwise?* For did not God say —when the first house was reared by Solomon—"I have hallowed this house. . . to put My name there *for ever;* and Mine eyes and My heart shall be there PERPETUALLY?" [4] There can be, then, I think, no doubt whatever, that when Paul spoke of "*the Man of Sin sitting in the Temple of God,*" he meant, that he should sit in a Temple *to be reared and dedicated unto God, the God of Israel, in Jerusalem,* where the Temple built by HEROD was *then* standing, and where that by SOLOMON had stood in days of old; the Temple in which God had put His name "FOR EVER." This proud opposer then must be a man YET TO BE REVEALED.

Again, He will ASSUME THE POSITION OF GOD. "He, *as God,* sitteth in the temple of God, *showing himself that* HE IS GOD." And this he will do *by a power not his*

_____
[1] Acts iii. 1.   [2] Acts xxi. 26.   [3] Acts xxiv. 11.   [4] 1 Kings ix. 3.

own, for we read that his "COMING IS AFTER THE WORKING (κατ' ἐνεργειαν, *i.e.,* after the *in*-working) *of Satan, with all power, and signs, and lying wonders, and with all deceivableness of unrighteousness."*

And again, THIS MAN WILL BE ALIVE WHEN CHRIST SHALL COME; for it is he "whom the Lord shall consume with the spirit of His mouth, and destroy with the brightness of His coming."

Thus does the Apostle speak of one to be revealed— "THAT MAN OF SIN,"—who will most certainly deserve the name of "ANTICHRIST."

To the same effect is the word of Daniel. In the eighth chapter we read of a vision in which the angel Gabriel addressed the prophet, saying, "Behold, I will make thee know what shall be in *the last end of the indignation.*" "When the transgressors are come to the full, a king of fierce countenance, and understanding dark sentences, shall stand up. And his power shall be mighty, but *not by his own power :* and he shall destroy wonderfully, and shall prosper and practise, and shall destroy the mighty and the holy people. And through his policy also he shall cause craft to prosper in his hand; and he shall *magnify himself in his heart, and by peace shall destroy many : he shall also stand up against the Prince of princes ; but he shall be broken without hand."* [1]

We find further corroboration in the eleventh chapter

---

[1] Dan. viii. 19-25.

of the same prophet. This chapter carries us through a course of events from the time of the Medes and Persians onwards, until the reign of a certain King, who, arising from a low estate—a vile person [1]—shall make a "league" with Israel,[2] "work deceitfully," "enter peaceably even upon the fattest places of the province, and do "that which his fathers have not done, nor his fathers' fathers." Of him we read further, " *he shall pollute the sanctuary of strength, and shall take away the daily sacrifice, and shall place the abomination that maketh desolate :* " he shall cause the people who "do know their God," and "understand," to "fall by the sword and by flame, by captivity and by spoil: . . . he shall do according to his will, and he shall *exalt himself, and magnify himself above every god, and shall speak marvellous things against the God of gods*, and shall prosper till the indignation be accomplished." "He shall plant the tabernacle of his palace between the seas in the glorious holy mountain ; yet he shall come to his end and none shall help him. *And at that time Michael shall stand up.* . . . And there shall be a time of trouble such as never was since there was a nation," and at that time shall the people written in God's book "be delivered," and the first resurrection (as explained before) [3] shall take place.[4]

[1] Dan. xi. 21.
[2] Comp. Dan. xi. 23 with Dan. ix. 27.
[3] See Chapter II.
[4] Dan. xi. 12.

Thus PAUL and DANIEL present for our contemplation a "MAN OF SIN" to be revealed in "the last time:" A MAN CLAIMING FOR HIMSELF THE HONOUR DUE TO THE ALMIGHTY, AND EXERCISING MORE THAN HUMAN POWER, BECAUSE INDWELT BY SATAN—A KING, MORE-OVER, STANDING UP AGAINST THE PRINCE OF PRINCES, TO BE DESTROYED WHEN HE APPEARS IN GLORY—AN ANTICHRIST, THEREFORE, INDEED.

I think that no candid reader will assert that such a man has reigned yet upon the earth. It is evidently *idle* to speak, as some have done, about Antiochus Epiphanes, or some chief oppressor among Roman emperors or leaders, or some Roman pontiff—or the Papacy itself. He who will examine honestly what Paul and Daniel have predicted, must surely be convinced that the king spoken of is a man—*one man*—of deep, dark mystery, who is YET TO BE REVEALED.

Having found so much information on the sacred page concerning the GREAT EVIL ONE who is to reign as king upon the earth, let us dwell for awhile on the POSITION and PECULIARITY of his kingdom and go-vernment, and we shall see clearly, I think, not only that he is an Antichrist, but THE GREAT ANTICHRIST especially foretold.

In the fourteenth chapter of Isaiah's prophecy we have BABYLON—*Babylon of the last days*—brought before us; the Babylon upon the overthrow of which the prophet says—"*the whole earth is at rest and is quiet, they break forth into singing.*" The burden of the chapter leaves no room for doubt that it is the same Babylon as that dwelt upon in the seventeenth and eighteenth chapters of REVELATION,—"that great city Babylon, that mighty city" with which the kings of the earth have committed fornication and lived deliciously; wherein is "merchandise of gold and silver, and precious stones, and pearls, and fine linen, and purple, . . . and odours, and ointments, and frankincense, and wine, and oil, . . . and chariots, and slaves, and souls of men,"—that "MYSTERY, BABYLON THE GREAT, THE MOTHER OF HARLOTS, AND ABOMINATIONS OF THE EARTH.

ISAIAH, in this fourteenth chapter, speaks much concerning the LAST KING of Babylon. He views that monarch at the end of his career, and says, "Hell from beneath is moved for thee, to meet thee at thy coming: it stirreth up the dead for thee." He portrays all the kings of the nations lying in their graves astonished at his overthrow. "Art thou become weak as we? Art thou become as one of us? How art thou fallen from heaven, O Lucifer, son of the morning! How art thou cut down to the ground which didst weaken the nations. For thou hast said in thine heart, I will ascend into heaven, I will exalt my throne above the stars of God;

I will ascend above the heights of the clouds; I will be *like the Most High.* Yet thou shalt be brought down to hell, to the sides of the pit. . . . The Lord of Hosts hath sworn, saying—Surely, as I have thought, so it shall come to pass; and as I have purposed, so shall it stand; that I will break the Assyrian in my land, and upon my mountains will I tread him under foot. Then shall his yoke depart from off them, and his burden depart from off their shoulders. This is the purpose that is purposed *upon the whole earth;* and this is the hand which is stretched out *upon all nations.*"

Such was the burden which Isaiah was commissioned to proclaim concerning this last monarch "in the year that King Ahaz died;" and thus, though not with the same fulness of detail, does he foretel his reign of terror in entire agreement both with Daniel and Paul, specifying, in prophetic symbol, the great nation he should rule, viz., the BABYLON of the *prophetic word: the* ROME *of history.*

But is it so? Are we right in thus deciding that his empire will be ROMAN? Let us carefully examine. Again we will refer to DANIEL, the seventh chapter. Herein we find laid down in order FOUR SEPARATE KINGDOMS bearing prominent rule in the world in different periods of its then future history. These kingdoms are exhibited under the emblems of four beasts with

distinguishing characteristics; and upon the expiration
of the time allotted to the fourth, a FIFTH kingdom is
brought forward, namely, "THE KINGDOM OF THE
PEOPLE OF THE SAINTS OF THE MOST HIGH." Now we
need hardly pause to explain to any who have sought
to 'understand their Bible, that there have been four
great empires, holding their dominion as the empires
of the world, beginning with the time of Daniel: the
BABYLONIAN, the MEDO-PERSIAN, the GRECIAN, and
the ROMAN. Dwelling upon the FOURTH of these
kingdoms, Daniel's prophecy informs us, that "it shall
be *diverse* from all kingdoms, and shall devour the whole
earth, and tread it down, and break it in pieces." That
such was the case with the ROMAN EMPIRE we know.

But further:—"The ten horns out of this kingdom
are *ten kings* that shall arise." It is remarkable that
from the very early times of the Christian era, down to
our own day, the number of kingdoms associated with
Rome has been *ten.* If we go back as far as the fourth
or fifth century, or if we descend to the eighth, the
twelfth, the sixteenth, or the nineteenth, we shall find
them to have been *ten,* until the late Italian war, when
the bond appears to have been broken,[1] for reasons

---

[1] Just before the war between France and Austria, when Napoleon III. took such an active part in the affairs of Italy, the kingdoms
or states *using the Latin tongue in their religious services,* and *bearing*

which we shall understand presently. But to pursue the language of the prophecy,—"And *another* (that is, another king) shall arise after them: and he shall be diverse from the first, and shall *subdue three kings.*" Now, surely, this seals the matter at once *against* THE PAPACY *being offered* to our notice, as represented by this last king. The Papacy cannot be justly said to have come after the ten kings, for it has reigned *with* or rather *over,* them; and, certainly, no historian can speak of it with emphasis, as having *subdued three kingdoms.* For this, we need but see how *greatly* commentators *differ* in their attempts to establish such a subjugation as a point of history. The eleventh king, then, cannot be the Papacy; and forasmuch as no king or headship answering these requirements has yet appeared, his reign *must* be still FUTURE. But further, —"He shall speak great swelling words against the Most High, and shall wear out the Saints of the Most High, and think to change times and laws; and they shall be given into his hand, until a time, and times, and the dividing of time. But the judgment shall sit, and they shall take away his dominion, to consume and to destroy it unto the end. And the kingdom and

allegiance to the Roman creed, were ten in number: France, Spain, Portugal, Austria, Sardinia, Tuscany, Modena, Parma, the States of the Church, and Naples.

dominion, and the greatness of the kingdom under the whole heaven, shall be given to the people of the Saints of the Most High."

Here then we have the period of this king's reign marked *definitely*. It shall be at the *close* of the time which is allotted to the *fourth great kingdom,* namely, the ROMAN.

But is this found to be clear also on reference to other parts of Scripture? We will refer to the following chapter (the eighth). In the nineteenth verse the period to which the grand point of the prophecy had reference, is distinctly named "THE LAST END OF THE INDIGNATION." Our attention is then directed to the kingdom of the Medes and Persians, and that of Alexander the Great, whose dominions were to be divided into four parts. (" *Four kingdoms shall stand up out of the nation, but not in his power.*"[1]) And passing on

---

[1] It may be well to call to memory what these four kingdoms were. The *first* was composed of Armenia, Media, Babylonia, Syria, Susiana, a portion of Cappadocia, and Cilicia. This kingdom, indeed, claimed an extension from India to the Hellespont. The *second* comprehended a part of Thrace, Asia Minor, part of Cappadocia, and the countries which were within the limits of Mount Taurus. The *third* consisted of Macedonia, Thessaly, and part of Greece. The *fourth* spread over part of Asia Minor, part of Thrace, Cœlo-Syria, Phœnicia, Palestine, Cyprus, Cyrene, and Egypt. The first kings were Alexander's four general's, Seleucus Nicator, Lysimachus, Cassander, and Ptolemy, who ruled over these four kingdoms respectively.

to the latter time of their kingdom when the transgressors are come to the full, we are told that "a king of fierce countenance, and understanding dark sentences, shall stand up," of whose character as delineated in this place we have already spoken. Now "THE LATTER TIME OF THEIR KINGDOM" must be the time of the fourth great kingdom of the world,—THE ROMAN: for the Romans gradually obtained dominion over all countries which the four joint successors of Alexander governed; Egypt (the last subjugated of the four) being made a province of the Roman Empire B.C. 30.

Thus, that the king of fierce countenance shall have dominion over the Roman Empire, is shown in *this* place also. But so far being clear from the testimony of the Prophets, let us seek for a more detailed account in the NEW TESTAMENT.

We will refer to REVELATION, the thirteenth chapter. This chapter is occupied with the affairs of "that great city Babylon, which reigneth over the kings of the earth." The Lord brings before us two allegorical figures, called "beasts." The first arises "out of the SEA." It has "SEVEN HEADS and TEN HORNS, and on its heads THE NAME OF BLASPHEMY." Now, there is certainly a great probability that ROME is represented by this figure—ROME IMPERIAL. ROME, the seat of the Empire, the point from which the Empire sprang, is situated *between the Seas.* It has had *seven forms of government* having their *seat* always at the ancient capital. These forms of government were as follows:— KINGS, CONSULS, DICTATORS, DECEMVIRS, CONSULAR TRIBUNES, EMPERORS, and POPES. And (as we have already seen) it has been peculiarly characterized by the association—at least for many centuries—of TEN KINGDOMS under its control, or closely bound to its interests. But we read that when "power, and a seat, and great authority" had been given by Satan to this Beast,—" *one of its heads was, as it were, wounded unto death ; and his deadly wound was healed,* and all the world wondered after the beast." This was true of Rome. The SIXTH head— that of the EMPERORS—was wounded unto death, by the sword of foreign invaders. It grew *weaker and weaker*, until the *name* of Emperor and no more existed. Yet, notwithstanding this, the nation did not actually *expire.* The capital was held by one who wore the diadem, as *King of all the Kings of Earth ;* and wonderful authority he exercised. The wounded beast *did live,* for the PAPACY kept it alive. It was indeed quite changed in character, and not acknowledged in the world as the old Roman Empire. Still it lived and flourished, for " *his deadly wound was healed ;* and all the world wondered after the beast. And they worshipped the dragon which gave power unto the beast ; and they worshipped the

beast saying, Who is like unto the Beast ? Who is able
to make war with him ?" And now again, we are told
"there was given unto him a mouth speaking great
things and blasphemies; and power was given unto him
to continue *forty and two months,* . . . . to make war
with the saints, and to overcome them ; and power was
given him over all kindreds, and tongues, and nations."
Now, if we accept (and there surely is no just reason
why we should not accept) the usual interpretation ; the
"forty and two months " are to be considered to be
months of *years ;* that is, *each day* therein is to be
reckoned *as a year.* Thus we have ONE THOUSAND TWO
HUNDRED AND SIXTY YEARS for the duration of the
Papacy as a headship of the Roman Empire. Now it
is worthy of remark certainly, and of serious thought
also, that from the Edict of Justinian (A.D. 533), which
gave political power to the Pope of Rome (and from the
date of which edict the Papal Empire grew with rapid
strides), to the well-known year 1793, when the Papacy
lost its imperial authority (and from which time it has
grown only more and more contemptible in a political
aspect), was *twelve hundred and sixty years,* or *forty and
two months.* The Papacy is still a power—alas ! but NOT
IMPERIAL. It has no authority which it can exercise
over any King in Europe. For this, its day is *gone.*
But let us see what is further stated in the Word before

us. "And I beheld ANOTHER BEAST coming up OUT OF THE EARTH; and he had *two horns* like a lamb, and he spake as a *dragon*. This second beast does not rise from the *sea;* his seat is not *Italy*, but INLAND; he comes up "OUT OF THE EARTH." He has "two horns like a lamb." The likeness to *a lamb* may indicate a remarkable appearance of *peacefulness;* while his speech being like that of *a dragon*, represents *cruelty*. The two horns may indicate a particular union of two kingdoms under the control of one headship. This "Lamb," it may be, "shall come in peaceably, and obtain the kingdom by flatteries," and "work deceitfully;"[1] so that "by peace he shall destroy many."[2] He is to "exercise all the power of the first beast before him;" that is, he is to be *head of the Roman Empire*, though his dwelling is not to be found between the seas. Moreover, he is to *do honour to the first beast*. He is to cause "the earth and them that dwell therein to *worship him;*" that is, we may suppose, to *bow down submissively to the Imperial authority* as of old. But more:—This new beast "*doeth wonders*, so that he maketh fire come down from heaven on the earth in the sight of men, *and deceiveth them that dwell on the earth by means of those miracles which he had power to do* IN THE SIGHT OF THE BEAST" (that is, in the sight of the *whole Empire*). And besides this, "he causeth all, both

---

[1] Dan. xi. 21-23.   [2] Dan. viii. 25.

small and great, rich and poor, free and bond, to receive
a mark in their right hand or in their foreheads; and
that no man might buy or sell save he that had the
mark or the name of the beast, or the number of his
name." And it is added—"Here is wisdom. Let him
that hath understanding count the number of the beast:
for it is the number of A MAN; and his number is, SIX
HUNDRED THREESCORE AND SIX."[1]

Now upon this second beast I will but comment
briefly. We know the dynasty which rose to power in
inland parts, and at the close of the last century laid
hands on the Imperial throne, taking all *but the name
only* from the Papacy; depriving him who held the
Imperial title by the Pope's authority, even of the empty
name in which he gloried.[2]

[1] Rev. xiii. It may be interesting to the reader to note that Irenæus
writing in the Second Century gives the following reckoning and
explanation of this mystical number. $\lambda = 30$, $a = 1$, $\tau = 300$, $\epsilon = 5$, $\iota = 10$,
$\nu = 50$, $o = 70$, $s = 200$, making up the total $= 666$; the letters together
spelling $\lambda a\tau\epsilon\iota\nu os$, a Latin person—a Roman.

[2] The Emperor Napoleon I. degraded the Pope to the rank of Bishop
of Rome, stripped the See of Rome of all its temporalities, and confis-
cated its revenues of every kind. The first blow was struck in 1793. In
1798, the blood of the Roman clergy was shed like water, the city of
Rome was taken, and the Pope (Pius VI.) was led away captive. In
1809, the temporal sovereignty of Rome and the States of the Church
was taken by General Radet, in the name of Napoleon, who divided the
States into departments, to be governed by French officers; and the
emperor conferred on his infant son the title of King of Rome. Thus

We have another very clear word upon this subject in the *seventeenth chapter.* A woman is spoken of "*sitting on many waters*" (the waters are elsewhere described as meaning "peoples, and multitudes, and nations, and tongues.")[1] The woman is arrayed in purple and scarlet, decked with gold, precious stones and pearls, having a golden cup in her hand, full of abominations, and upon her forehead a name written— MYSTERY, BABYLON THE GREAT, THE MOTHER OF HARLOTS, AND ABOMINATIONS OF THE EARTH." She appears "drunken with the blood of the saints and the martyrs of Jesus." Now every one reading this description of the woman, is ready to decide at once "THIS IS THE PAPACY." And no doubt *it is so.* But it is NOT "The Antichrist." It is NOT "The Man of Sin." It may be a *type* of him, but it is *not he.* Let us observe what is said about the woman, for it is worth our close attention. In the third verse we read thus,—"He carried me away into *the wilderness;* and I saw the woman *sit upon a scarlet-coloured beast.*" Her place and position, therefore, are *changed.* She *had been* "sitting upon MANY WATERS" (*i.e., ruling over many nations*).

---

the Papacy, as an Imperial power, received a blow, from which it has not rallied.—See *Hale's Chronology,* vol. iii. p. 625, 626 ; and *Keith's World and Church,* p. 214–217.

[1] Rev. xvii. 15.

But *now* she has *left her* position of authority, and we find her *in the wilderness, supported by a scarlet-coloured beast,* full of names of blasphemy, having SEVEN HEADS and TEN HORNS; she is supported, therefore, by the same beast which came before us as the *first* beast in the *thirteenth chapter*—namely, THE ROMAN EMPIRE. Then we have here THE ROMAN EMPIRE SUPPORTING THE PAPACY; the Papacy, as it would appear, *having become too weak to support itself.* But an explanation is afforded us in this chapter, which makes it very plain that only the *last headship* of this Empire is the actual supporter. In the *seventh verse* we find the Angel saying,—"I will tell thee the mystery of the woman, and of the beast that carrieth her, which hath the seven heads and ten horns. The beast that thou sawest WAS, and IS NOT; and shall ascend out of the bottomless pit, and go into perdition : and they that dwell on the earth shall wonder, whose names were not written in the book of life from the foundation of the world, when they behold THE BEAST THAT WAS AND IS NOT, AND YET IS. And here is the mind that hath wisdom. The *seven heads* are seven mountains, on which the woman sitteth " (Rome is built on seven hills). "And there are seven kings " (this we have explained already). "Five are fallen." (In the day of the vision five of the forms of government had passed away ; viz.,

Kings, Consuls, Dictators, Decemvirs, and Consular-
Tribunes.) "One *is*." (The form of government in
the time of the Apostle John was Imperial; Emperors
ruled.) "And the other is not yet come, and when he
cometh he must *continue* a short space." (When the
Empire was wounded unto death, the Papacy took the
reins of government, stepping in gradually to take its
place, and heal the wound, and soon, assuming full
imperial functions, gave away kingdoms, and treated
kings as vassals. It continued forty and two months,
that is—taking a day for a year—TWELVE HUNDRED
AND SIXTY YEARS, when it likewise was compelled to
resign the throne and give way to another power).
"And the BEAST THAT WAS, AND IS NOT, even he is the
eighth and is *of the seven*" (he does not *seem* to be of the
seven; he is not *called* either Emperor, or Pope, or
King, but he is in truth THE HEAD nevertheless).

But what have we here? A dynasty RISING INTO
POWER; then PASSING AWAY; and then RISING AGAIN.
As to this dynasty, we have but one word further. It
is joined, like the Empire of old, by TEN KINGS, and they
make war with the Lamb; and unite together also to
consume the Papacy which they had supported. They
conspire, in fact, to cast out of the world ALL RELIGION,
except that idol-worship, THAT WORSHIP OF THE BEAST
HIMSELF, which he will set up " in the temple of God,"

where he will show himself that "*he is God;*" and
finally, having fulfilled his day like those who preceded
him, he shall "GO INTO PERDITION" together with the
"FALSE PROPHET" who will work miracles before him;
to be followed in God's own good time by the remaining
person of the antichristian trinity, — THE DRAGON
(SATAN), who must be reserved a little while, though
bound, and by a lengthy bondage kept from carrying on
his work of evil. Apart then from the help we might
derive from the prophetic *dates*, we can perceive without
much room for doubt, *if any*, from WHAT QUARTER we
must look for the LAST KING; the Great Opponent of
the Lord; the "Idol Shepherd;" the Great Deceiver;
"the Antichrist." It is evident that he pertains to
the EIGHTH DYNASTY OF THE ROMAN HEADSHIP; the
dynasty which rose in 1793, and quickly established
itself upon the ground long occupied by the Imperial
Popes. But observe the remarkable fact, that this
dynasty yielded up its power and "WAS NOT" in 1815—
the British arms prevailing on the field of Waterloo,—
but which rose again—and so "YET WAS" in 1848,
laying the old hand on Rome. Nevertheless, again the
dynasty "WAS NOT" in 1870, and "IS NOT" still, nor
shall be for a period, how long, God only knows, but
again SHALL BE, that it may go into perdition. Therefore we may safely think we are not *very* far from THAT

GREAT DAY, WHEN EVERY BELIEVER SHALL BEHOLD HIS LORD.

But now there is another point which we must notice, before we quit this subject of the *reign of Antichrist*. I mean, HIS DEALINGS WITH THE JEWISH PEOPLE, of whose restoration we were led to speak particularly in the earlier part of this chapter.

We must refer once more to DANIEL's prophecy. Much difference has arisen among prophetical interpreters concerning the SEVENTY WEEKS spoken of in the *ninth chapter*. It is said "SEVENTY WEEKS are determined upon thy people, and upon thy holy city, to finish the transgression, and to make an end of sins, and to make reconciliation for iniquity, and to bring in everlasting righteousness, and to seal up the vision and prophecy, and to anoint the Most Holy." Observe this carefully, " *Seventy weeks* " (taking, as the necessity of the case obliges, a day for a year; equal therefore to *four hundred and ninety years*) "are determined " (נחתך cut off, divided) "upon *thy* people" (Daniel's people, the Jews), "and upon *thy* holy city" (Jerusalem), "to finish " (כלא shut up, restrain) "the transgression " (*i.e.*, of thy people and city), "and to make an end of" (חתם to seal up) "sins, and to make reconciliation for" (כפר to cover) "iniquity, and to bring in everlasting righteousness, and to seal up the vision and the

prophecy, and to anoint the Most Holy," (קדש קדשים
Whether this expression refers to *the "Holy of Holies"*
in the Temple, or to *the Messiah Himself*, does not
appear certain; but it is only right to state that if it
have reference to the *Messiah*, it is *the only case* in
which this expression, which is used in nearly *thirty
places* in the Old Testament, is applied to a person).

Now we know well that scarcely any of these points
can yet be looked upon as fulfilled. *The transgression
of the Jews* is not by any means *restrained, shut up, or
finished :* for they reject the Lord as firmly as they ever
did, and as truly do they glory in denying Him. *Their
sins* are not *sealed up*, nor *made an end of*, but they are
as patent to all the world as are the sins of the Gentiles.
Reconciliation truly is *offered*, because the atonement is
complete through the sacrifice of Christ, but it is not
made. There is not reconciliation yet between the Lord
and Israel: their *iniquity* is not *covered*, though the
covering is all in readiness. *Everlasting righteousness* is
not *brought in* amongst the tribes of Israel, for hitherto
they have made choice of sin. *The vision and prophecy*
are not yet fulfilled, nor sealed, but open, as of old, to
the expectation of God's waiting people. *The Holy of
Holies* is not yet *anointed*, for their temple is *not yet
erected.* So I CANNOT THINK, with some interpreters,
that the SEVENTY WEEKS HAVE YET EXPIRED. But let

H

us follow onward with the subject. "Know therefore and understand," said the angel, "that from the going forth of the commandment to restore and rebuild Jerusalem unto Messiah the Prince, shall be seven weeks and threescore and two weeks" (that is, four hundred and eighty-three years, taking, as before, a day to represent a year), . . . "And after threescore and two weeks SHALL MESSIAH BE CUT OFF, BUT NOT FOR HIMSELF." This brings us to *a definite period*— the cutting off of Messiah : *the crucifixion of our Lord.* What then was to follow? The Word continues, "And the people of the prince that shall come shall destroy the city and the sanctuary." Now we know that the people who destroyed Jerusalem and its Temple were ROMANS. THE PRINCE REFERRED TO WAS THEREFORE TO BE A ROMAN ALSO. But further it is said—"And the end thereof shall be with a flood, and unto the end of the war desolations are determined." And it *was so* ASSUREDLY. But here the matter has been resting ever since. The war ended in the dispersion of the sons of Judah till the times of the Gentiles should be fulfilled. But with the Gentiles, nay, with *Christians* (as such), this prophecy has *nothing whatever to do.* The seventy weeks were determined upon *Daniel's people*—the Jews—*and no other.* In looking, therefore, for the *remaining week*—THE LAST OF THE SEVENTY—we must keep our eyes upon the day, *yet future,* when "the times of the Gentiles" shall have been accomplished. Then shall "THE PRINCE" of that people which before-time destroyed the city and the Temple come forward on the behalf of Israel. "And he shall confirm the (a) covenant with many for *one week:* and *in the midst of the week* he shall cause the sacrifice and the oblation to cease, and for the over-spreading of abominations he shall make it desolate *even until the consummation.*" The Prince, then, who will make the covenant must be a DECEIVER,—*one who will not keep his word.* He will make a covenant with all the appearance of strength and security for seven years, and *break it in the midst of the time, that he may overspread the land with abominations, and until the end appointed make it desolate.* Who now shall this Roman Prince or leader be, who shall act thus towards Israel? Who indeed but that DREAD BEING, that "MAN OF SIN" of whom we have been speaking.

Surely, then, we have a hint as to the meaning of our Saviour's words, "IF ANOTHER SHALL COME IN HIS OWN NAME, HIM YE WILL RECEIVE."[1] This last head of the Roman Empire will probably be THE FALSE MESSIAH OF THE JEWS, and thus, in very perfect sense, "THE ANTI-CHRIST." But now, the covenant made,—the Jews brought to their land under his protection,—the Temple and the

---

[1] John v. 43.

sacrificial rites restored: and now *again* the *covenant broken*, and the sacrifice and oblation caused to cease in the midst of the seven years: THREE YEARS AND A HALF ("a time, times, and the dividing of time," as Daniel predicted,[1]) are left for the full display of all the horrors of the Antichrist's dominion: his gross unparalleled idolatry, his bitter cruelty, his craft, his thirst for blood. Then he shall come to his end; for MICHAEL, the great Prince, shall stand up for *Israel's remnant.* Yea, the Lord shall come, and all His Saints attending Him, and this "Man of Sin" shall be consumed. But the destruction of Antichrist and the reception of Israel's remnant by the Lord Jesus must be reserved for the next chapter. To enter upon them would oblige us to bring forward matter which has properly to do with the subjects next in order, viz.: THE ADVENT, AND THE JUDGMENT OF THE NATIONS.

Let it suffice for the present that Israel will be indeed restored, *at least in part,* and that in UNBELIEF, *under the auspices of* ANTICHRIST; that they will erect their Temple and restore their ancient worship; but that their protector will turn speedily against them, and they will endure a tribulation of a kind more bitter than all former trials.

In concluding this chapter, let me impress upon my

[1] Dan. vii. 25.

readers THE GREAT NEED OF PRAYER ON THE BEHALF OF ISRAEL. We have seen already, and in the next chapter shall see more particularly, what great blessings God has laid up in store for the Twelve Tribes in the Millennial age. But they have *much to suffer first*. We must, then, keep them in remembrance.

Moreover, while we pray for them, let us look well also AT HOME; examining OUR OWN standing before God. For even now are there many Antichrists: forerunners of "THE ANTICHRIST" who shall appear. INFIDELITY is an Antichrist: POPERY and TRACTARIANISM are Antichrists: ULTRA-CHURCHISM and DENOMINATIONALISM are ANTICHRISTS: ANTINOMIANISM is an Antichrist: LUKEWARMNESS is an Antichrist. Let us see that we take not the side of any such, but ever guard our hearts with prayer and watchfulness; ever keep our lives in harmony with the inspired Word: ever KEEP OUR BEST AFFECTIONS FIXED WITH FIRMNESS ON THE SAVIOUR. So, when the world's iniquity is headed up in the person of THE GREAT ANTICHRIST, he will have no part in us.

CHAPTER IV.

The Advent.

"Behold, He cometh with clouds, and every eye shall see Him, and they also which pierced Him; and all kindreds of the Earth shall wail because of Him. Even so. Amen."—REV. i. 7.

IT will be needful for us to retrace our steps a little, in order that we may deal fairly with the subject which now comes before us. That subject is THE ADVENT.

Uplifting first the mind towards heaven, we must behold our Great Redeemer, there enthroned in glory at the right hand of the Eternal Father. He is a Man, bone of our bone, and flesh of our flesh; a Man who once was dead, but liveth, and has been exalted above all the Principalities and Powers of Heaven; a Man, before whose GLORIFIED HUMANITY the angels bow. A Man, yet God:[1] the very and Eternal God, "for whom are all things, and by whom all things consist."[2] Since, in the sight of His disciples He ascended up on high,

---

[1] John i. 1-3; Rom. ix. 5.　　　　[2] Col. i. 16, 17.

His Session has been there: and there, amid unceasing praises, He must sit—the great High Priest—the only "Mediator between God and men"—until the day appointed by the Father, when He shall descend once more to Earth for JUDGMENT and SALVATION.

In heaven, then, at the right hand of power, awaiting the appointed time, let us BEHOLD OUR LORD as we commence this Chapter. And let us note well the fact, —*He shall descend to earth again.* HE shall descend. That once despised and rejected Lord, who by the hand of wickedness was crucified, but who by the Eternal Spirit rose again, and then ascended, and now sits enthroned at the right hand of power—THAT VERY JESUS, at the time appointed, SHALL DESCEND, as King and Judge, UPON OUR FALLEN EARTH.

Moreover, it is evident that he will come AS MAN; clothed indeed in the *perfection* of our manhood, but still in its *reality.* It does not require much searching into Scripture to establish this. In the *first chapter* of THE ACTS OF THE APOSTLES we are told that when Jesus had spoken His last words to His disciples, "while they beheld, He was taken up, and a cloud received Him out of their sight. And while they looked stedfastly toward heaven, as He went up, behold two men stood by them in white apparel, which said, Ye men of Galilee, why stand ye gazing up into heaven?

THIS SAME JESUS which is taken up from you into
heaven, shall *so come in like manner as ye have seen Him
go into heaven*." "THIS SAME JESUS," then, who had
arisen from the grave, who had been crucified, who had
dwelt and ministered among the sons of men; who had
been born of a human mother in Bethlehem;—THIS
SAME JESUS shall most surely come again "*in like
manner*" as He went. *Descending*, instead of *ascending;*
the clouds unfolding to *reveal* His manhood, instead of
closing round about *to hide it* from our sight.

Let us follow the ALMIGHTY SAVIOUR by the steps
of His descent.

"The MAN JESUS CHRIST" quits the Throne of
Intercession at the right hand of Heaven, and advances
towards the earth. The glory of the Father's Majesty
surrounds Him. The Holy Angels bear Him company.[1]
Thus, to an appointed place in heights above the world,
He makes descent, and there *a pause ensues*.[2] The
trumpet sounds in the hearing of the DEAD *in Christ*,
that they arise from grave, and tomb, and earth, and
stream, and sea, to meet Him. It sounds, moreover, in
the hearing of the LIVING SAINTS, that their frail mortal
put on immortality, and that they ascend to be for ever
with the Lord. And all who hear obey the summons.
On this "first resurrection" we have dwelt before; we

---

[1] Matt. xxv. 31; Mark viii. 38.   [2] Thess. iv. 16, 17; Rev. xix.

need not speak of it, therefore, in further explanation. THUS, however, does the LAST GREAT DAY—the DAY OF THE LORD'S ADVENT—open.

But, when the multitudes who have arisen and ascended to their Lord are in His presence, *what shall follow?* Surely eye of man hath never seen, nor ear heard, nor heart conceived—the JOY, the BLISS, the GLORY! Oh, think of the re-union of those loving] ones the grave has so long severed! Husbands and wives, parents and children, friends and friends, united now to live and love FOR EVER! No more to shed a tear! no more to doubt, nor sin, nor suffer! No friend to cause another pang of grief to friend! The name of enemy unknown! All perfect peace, rest, joy, praise, glory, *everlastingly*. And then the brightness—Oh, the brightness of the Hosts of Heaven!—those HOLY ANGELS, close attendants on the King of kings, each one so beautiful, so good, so full of love! To have such beings for companions! To converse with them of all the marvels of redeeming grace! To hear their words declare the praises of *their* Lord and *ours!* How wonderful! But then again—more glorious still—The vision of the great ALMIGHTY KING! "The King in His beauty!" "The altogether lovely!" To gaze upon His glory *now* would be beyond endurance. But *then* we shall have power to look upon His face, and "see

Him as He is," arrayed in all the brightness of the Father's glory. Then too shall we *praise Him* as the angels praise, and *love Him* with a love which those alone can feel whose once sin-ruined souls have been redeemed and saved.

But let us glance just for a moment at OURSELVES as we shall be when thus we look upon, and love, and praise Him. OURSELVES—*in new array—how changed! how wholly changed!* This frail corruption having put on incorruption, and this weak mortal, immortality,[1] we shall no longer bear the stamp of sin, or its sad consequences, but we shall be LIKE THE LORD. It is not said we shall be like the *angels*, but we shall be like *the Lord*—LIKE CHRIST![2] Yes, since we are washed in His blood, clothed in His righteousness, made holy by His Spirit, complete in Him : "SONS, moreover, in His Sonship; HEIRS in His Heirship; KINGS in His Kingship; PRIESTS in his Priesthood, we shall be GLORIFIED TOGETHER WITH HIM IN HIS OWN TRANSCENDENT GLORY."[3] Oh, what a blissful sequel to the toils and griefs of earth! *Can we now see our title clearly to this blessed state?* Would this glory be *our* portion, think we, if the Lord were to come NOW? If not,—*Oh, why not?* Not because of any want of love or grace on GOD'S

---

[1] 1 Cor. xv. 53.   [2] 1 John iii. 2.

[3] John xvii. 22 ; Rom. viii. 14–17 ; Rev. i. 6 ; iii. 21.

part. Far from it; for there is a FULL and FREE SAL-
VATION, through the faith of Jesus, offered to each
sinner upon Earth. Christ died *for all*, and God wills
all men to be saved.[1] Search the Scriptures; see
if such a thing *can be* as a Believer in Christ Jesus *lost*.
Nay, you will search *in vain*. IT CANNOT BE, thank
God. "As Moses lifted up the serpent in the wilderness,
even so is the Redeemer lifted up, that WHOSOEVER
BELIEVETH IN HIM should not perish, but have everlasting life."[2] LET US BELIEVE THEN—fellow travellers
to eternity—BELIEVE IN THE LORD JESUS CHRIST, AND
WE SHALL LIVE; yea, LIFE IS OURS,—a life which cannot
end. This is the PRESENT—the IMMEDIATE—portion of
the weakest "child of faith,"[3] and the glory of JOINT-
HEIRSHIP follows speedily.

In this estate of glory we must leave the Saints of
Jesus for the present, that we may observe some of the
great events which will take place upon the earth.

If not *before* the resurrection and translation of the
Church of Christ,[4] at any rate *soon after* they are
gathered to their Lord, the Reign of the last king, as
ANTICHRIST, will commence, and the persecution of the
Saints upon the Earth be set on foot. The Jews will

---

[1] 2 Cor. v. 14, 15; 2 Tim. ii. 4; Heb. ii. 9.
[2] John iii. 14, 15.   [3] John iii. 36; vi. 47; xi. 25, 26.
[4] See Chapter II.

then discover their grand error: the covenant will be broken; and "the day of Jacob's trouble" be revealed. God, by the hand of Antichrist, will have gathered them into Jerusalem, and will blow upon them in the fire of His wrath, and melt them in the midst thereof.

And the distress will be *effectual:* for the Spirit of Grace and Supplication will be poured upon them from Heaven, and they will look on Him "whom they have pierced, and mourn for Him, as one mourneth for his only son, and be in bitterness for Him, as one that is in bitterness for his first-born. In that day there shall be a great mourning in Jerusalem, ... and the land shall mourn, every family apart; . . . . *all the families that remain*, every family apart, and their wives apart." And " in that day there shall be a fountain opened to the house of David and to the inhabitants of Jerusalem, for sin and for uncleanness." And God will bring *a third part* through the fire, and will refine them as silver is refined, and will try them as gold is tried; they shall call on His name, and He will hear them; He will say, " *It is My people ;*" and they shall say, " *The Lord is my God.*"[1] Thus, as Zechariah informs us, the remnant of Israel will be brought to repentance at the last hour, and be permitted, *at the very Advent itself*, to look on Him whom they pierced, and obtain life through His

[1] Zech. xii. 10–14; xiii. 1, 2.

name. There will "in that day" be a fountain open for sin "to the house of David and to the inhabitants of Jerusalem," *and the destroying angel will allow the third of those among God's covenanted people who had been deceived by Antichrist, to live.* They will be left amongst the remnant whom the Lord will spare, to people the millennial earth.

Another great event is brought before us in connection with the Saviour's Advent, namely, THE DESTRUCTION OF BABYLON " "THE MYSTERY." The exact position of Great Babylon's overthrow with respect to the time of Israel's trouble and the Advent of the Lord is, I think, clear. It will be *immediately* upon the manifestation of Antichrist as the great idolater, and the persecutor of God's people. That is to say—it will be only *three years and a half at most* before the Lord's descent upon the Earth. But we must dwell upon this stroke of desolation for an instant.

In the fourteenth chapter of the REVELATION we find "the first-fruits unto God and to the Lamb" brought before us assembled together with Christ on Mount Zion, and following Him withersoever He goeth.[1] Then we have the word of exhortation uttered by an angel's voice to every nation, and kindred, and tongue, and

[1] See *The Book of Revelation in Diagram.* Note upon "The Orders of Saints."

people, "Fear God, and give glory to Him; for the hour of His judgment is come," which we have before alluded to as having probable reference to *a great revival of religion* following immediately upon the removal of the Lord's people from the Earth. In the next verse we find the statement—"And there followed another angel, saying, 'BABYLON IS FALLEN, IS FALLEN, THAT GREAT CITY, BECAUSE SHE MADE ALL NATIONS DRINK OF THE WINE OF THE WRATH OF HER FORNICATION.'" Then *another* angel follows, saying with a loud voice—"If any man worship the beast and his image, and receive his mark in his forehead or in his hand, the same shall drink of the wine of the wrath of God." The proclamation concerning the fall of Babylon, coming, as it does, *after* the intimations of the first resurrection and the revival of religion—and *before* the solemn warning respecting the beast and his image, suggests that although the overthrow of the great city will take place at the *beginning* of Antichrist's reign, it will be *before* or *immediately upon,* the full development of his true character; and about synchronize with the commencement of Israel's great tribulation.

But the eighteenth chapter affords more exact particulars about this overthrow. We find there a warning voice from heaven—"Come out of her (*i.e.,* Babylon), My people, that ye be not partakers of her sins, and that ye receive not of her plagues. . . . . Her plagues shall come in one day, death, and mourning, and famine : and she shall be utterly burned with fire; for strong is the Lord God who judgeth her. . . . . *In one hour* is thy judgment come. . . . . Rejoice over her, thou heaven, and ye holy apostles and prophets; for God hath avenged you on her. And a mighty angel took up a stone like a great millstone, and cast it into the sea, saying, Thus with violence shall that great city Babylon be thrown down, and shall be found no more at all. . . . . And in her was found the blood of prophets, and of saints, and of all that were slain upon the earth." So does the word of prophecy foretel the sudden and entire overthrow of "Babylon the Great," which we have shown, I think, beyond all doubt, is ROME.[1] Whether by what is said we are to understand that ROME—THE ACTUAL CITY—will be suddenly destroyed by fire; or whether the iniquitous POWER OF THE PAPACY which has its rule in this city as its great centre, is referred to, is not perhaps quite clear. But there is sufficient evidence to afford strong *probability* that the destruction of the *actual city* is intended : for if we refer to the account given of the overthrow of *the Papacy*, in the seventeenth chapter of Revelation,[2] we find that the overthrow of the "city," in the light of *a power* " *which reigneth over the*

[1] See Chapter III.   [2] Rev. xvii. 15–16.

kings of the earth," will be a *gradual* work brought about by the hatred of Antichrist and his ten kings ; whereas *this* destruction is to be *sudden*—the work of "*one hour,*" —and "the kings of the earth" who were brought before us as the DESTROYERS in the *former* case, are declared in *this latter* to BEWAIL her, and LAMENT for her, when they see the smoke of her burning.[1] Surely, moreover, there was a fulness of meaning when the "mighty angel took up a stone like a great millstone, and cast it into the sea, saying, Thus *with violence* shall that great city Babylon be thrown down, and shall be found no more at all. And the voice of harpers and musicians shall be heard no more at all in thee ; and no craftsman, of whatsoever craft he be, shall be found any more in thee ; . . . . and the light of a candle shall shine no more at all in thee ; and the voice of the bridegroom and of the bride shall be heard no more at all in thee." Reason would that we should conclude *almost positively,* since we have such a word as this, that when, through the hatred of Antichrist and his ten kings, the *Papal power* shall have been overthrown, the Lord Himself will take the judgment of the CITY into His own hand, and *with a flood of fire* DESTROY IT UTTERLY.

The work of judgment on THE CITY OF SUCH BITTER PERSECUTIONS AND EXCEEDING WRONGS, will not pass

---

[1] Rev. xviii. 9, 10.

unobserved by those who are IN HEAVEN. The risen
Saints with Christ will see, and utter praise immediately.
For mark how the next chapter opens—"And after
these things, I heard a great voice of much people in
heaven, saying, Alleluia; Salvation, and glory, and
honour, and power, unto the Lord our God; for true
and righteous are His judgments; for He hath judged
the great whore, which did corrupt the earth with her
fornication, and hath avenged the blood of His servants
at her hand. And again they said, Alleluia; and her
smoke rose up for ever and ever."[1]

But they have more to witness yet, ere they descend
from the expanse above, with the Almighty Judge, to
earth. There must be more judgments on the wicked:
and the last great tribulation of the Church of that brief
dispensation and of Israel also, must receive the completion of its measure, that their cup of sorrow may be
filled unto repentance.

Again: When the great Harlot City Babylon is
fallen, and the warning voice is uttered by the angel,
"If any man worship the beast or his image . . . . he
shall drink of the wine of the wrath of God, . . . and . .
be tormented with fire and brimstone in the presence
of the holy angels and in the presence of the Lamb;"—
then the Saints who yet adorn the earth are spoken of:

[1] Rev. xix. 1-3.

for the day of their "patience" has come; a voice is heard from Heaven, bidding the Apostle "write— Blessed are the dead which die in the Lord from hence- forth: yea, saith the Spirit, that they may rest from their labours, and their works do follow them:"[1] and immediately we find the Lord, "the Son of Man," *en- throned upon a white cloud, prepared to reap and gather the abundant harvest.* By which I suppose we are to learn that a persecution unto death, which has not known a precedent, shall cut down its thousands, who will be added to the shining throngs above, till the whole earth is reaped and the whole harvest gathered. Thus the "great multitude, which no man could number, out of all nations, and kindreds, and people, and tongues,"[2] will be made up, prepared to stand before the Throne of God and of the Lamb. They will "have come out of great tribulation" (ἐκ τῆς θλίψεως τῆς μεγάλης, out of *the* tribulation *the great one*), and shall stand before the throne for ever. But when the whole number shall be thus completed, and all the subjects of the Saviour's kingdom gathered; then the "voice from the throne" will be heard, saying, "Praise our God, all ye His servants, and ye that fear Him, both small and great." And the Apostle adds, "I heard as it were the voice of a great multitude, and as the voice of many waters, and

---

[1] Rev. xiv. 12, 13. [2] Rev. vii. 9–17.

as the voice of mighty thundering, saying, Alleluia; for the Lord God omnipotent reigneth. Let us be glad and rejoice, and give honour to Him: for the marriage of the Lamb is come, and His wife hath made herself ready."[1] And now the whole Church—the Bride of Christ—appears before Him in the vision clothed in fine linen, clean and white: no member wanting: no trembling, weak disciple left unheeded: but the entire body of believers, gathered in one blissful throng, rejoicing with exceeding joy because the last great tribulation of the Church is finished, and eternal glory is the only portion now remaining to the sainted sufferers.

While it shall be thus in Heaven, what will be the state of things *on Earth?* Our Lord Himself has told us that great signs and wonders are to be beheld. "The sun shall be darkened, the moon shall not give her light, the stars shall fall from heaven, and the powers of heaven shall be shaken." Let me remark here that these signs in heaven are nowhere spoken of as taking place till "*after*" the last great tribulation. In MATTHEW the word concerning this is very plain: "IMMEDIATELY AFTER *the tribulation of those days* shall the sun be darkened and the moon shall not give her light, and the stars shall fall from heaven, and the powers of heaven shall be shaken, and *then*," it is added, "shall appear the

[1] Rev. xix. 6, 7.

sign of the Son of man in heaven."[1] MARK speaks plainly also,—" But in those days, *after* that tribulation, the sun shall be darkened, and the moon shall not give her light, and the stars of heaven shall fall, and the powers that are in heaven shall be shaken. And then shall they see the Son of man coming in the clouds."[2] In LUKE we find the exact period of these wonders to be that in which the completion of "the times of the Gentiles" shall be arrived at. He informs us that the same remarkable incidents which are mentioned both by MATTHEW and MARK will come to pass; but with these additions—" upon the earth distress of nations, with perplexity; the sea and the waves roaring; men's hearts failing them for fear, and for looking after those things which are coming on the earth."[3]

At the time, then, WHEN THE TRIBULATION SHALL HAVE DONE ITS WORST AGAINST GOD'S PEOPLE of that dispensation, shall these signs and wonders be revealed.

But though the hand of *persecution* will be stayed for want of saints to persecute,—the hand of *cruelty and bloodshed* will be lifted up with power. Upon the earth will be " *distress of nations, with perplexity.*"

And further, it is evident that at that time JERUSALEM WILL BE THE CENTRE OF THE FEARFUL WARFARE. There will Antichrist "plant the tabernacle of his

[1] Matt. xxiv. 29, 30.　　[2] Mark xiii. 24–26.　　[3] Luke xxi. 24–27.

palace." There will be THE SEAT OF THE LAST STRUGGLE
BETWEEN ALL THE POWERS OF EARTH. Against that
Holy City will all nations of the earth be gathered to
"THE BATTLE OF THE GREAT DAY OF GOD ALMIGHTY."

Important details with regard to this are found
in the Prophet DANIEL. He brings before us the last
king—that *wilful one*—having his seat in Palestine, and
dividing the land "for gain." He then tells us how
that "at the time of the end shall the King of the
South push at him, and the King of the North shall
come against him like a whirlwind, . . . and tidings out
of the east and out of the north shall trouble him;"
wherefore "he shall go forth with great fury to destroy
and utterly to make away many; *and he shall plant
the tabernacle of his palace between the seas in the glorious
Holy Mountain.*"[1]

JOEL, too, speaks of the troubles of that time when
"the day of the Lord cometh . . . and is nigh at
hand," the day when "the earth shall quake, . . .
the heavens shall tremble, and the sun and the moon
shall be dark, and the stars shall withdraw their
shining,"—and declares that "in those days" . . .
the Lord "will gather all nations, and will bring them
to the *valley of Jehoshaphat,* and plead with them
there." . . . "Proclaim ye this among the Gentiles,—

[1] Dan. xi. 39–45.

prepare war, wake up the mighty men, . . . beat your
plowshares into swords, and your pruning-hooks into
spears: let the weak say, I am strong. Assemble
yourselves and come all ye heathen, and gather
yourselves together round about: *thither* cause thy
mighty ones to come down, O Lord. Let the
heathen be awakened, and come up to the *valley of
Jehoshaphat :* for *there* will I sit to judge all the
heathen round about. . . . Multitudes, multitudes, in
the valley of decision; for the day of the Lord is near
in the valley of decision. The sun and the moon shall
be darkened, and the stars shall withdraw their shining."

ZECHARIAH likewise testifies, "Behold, *I will make
Jerusalem a cup of trembling* unto all the people round
about, when they shall be in the siege, both *against
Judah and against Jerusalem.* And in that day, *I will
make Jerusalem a burdensome stone for all people ;* all
that burden themselves with it shall be cut in pieces,
though all the people of the earth be gathered together
against it. . . . . Behold, the day of the Lord cometh,
and thy spoil shall be divided in the midst of thee.
For *I will gather all nations against Jerusalem to battle ;*
and the city shall be taken, . . . and half of the city
shall go forth into captivity, and the residue of the
people shall not be cut off from the city. Then shall
the Lord go forth, . . . *and His feet shall stand in that*

day upon the Mount of Olives, which is before Jerusalem on the east; .... and the Lord my God shall come, and all the Saints."[1]

THUS JERUSALEM SHALL BE THE GRAND CENTRE OF THE EARTH'S AFFLICTION WHEN THE DAY OF THE LORD'S COMING IS AT HAND.

Perhaps it may have surprised some persons that I have not referred to the (so-called) "BATTLE OF ARMAGEDDON," while speaking of the final acts of warfare near Jerusalem. Let me explain this omission.

I do not think that a battle *properly called* "the Battle of Armageddon" will take place. If we look at the sixteenth chapter of REVELATION (which is the only place in the whole Bible in which ARMAGEDDON is brought before us) we shall not find any *Battle* of Armageddon spoken of, but simply A GATHERING TOGETHER OF THE KINGS OF THE EARTH, *through the instrumentality of evil spirits,* at a place called ARMAGEDDON, in readiness for "THE BATTLE OF THE GREAT DAY OF GOD ALMIGHTY;" which battle, as we have already seen, is to be fought in the immediate neighbourhood of JERUSALEM.

It will hardly be said that JERUSALEM was spoken of as "a place called in the *Hebrew tongue*—ARMAGEDDON :" for "*Jerusalem*" is itself a *Hebrew* name. Some other

[1] Zech. xii. 2-4 ; xiv. 1-5.

place than this must be intended.[1] A *gathering*, however, at *some* place so called, if rendered in the Hebrew
tongue, there will be. It will be, perhaps, a congress of
kings, held at the place, to decide on matters with
regard to Eastern territories—matters of importance to
the nations generally; a congress called by *Antichrist*
in subtlety, so that by the semblance of peace, many
may be destroyed. But observe the language of Scripture in this place—"I saw three unclean spirits, like
frogs, come out of the mouth of the dragon, and out of
the mouth of the beast, and out of the mouth of the
false prophet; for they are the spirits of devils, working
miracles, which go forth unto the kings of the earth and
of the whole world, to gather them to the battle of the
great day of God Almighty." Then a word of solemn
warning follows—"Behold, I come as a thief. Blessed
is he that watcheth and keepeth his garments, lest he
walk naked, and they see his shame." This warning
being uttered, the prophetic history proceeds—"And he
gathered them together into a place called in the
Hebrew tongue Armageddon."

[1] There are different opinions as to the etymology of Armageddon.
Some suppose it to be composed of the two words, עָר a city, and מכד
something very noble. Others tell us it should be הָר a mountain,
and מגר; others, again, that it is either עָר or חָר and מגדו Megiddo.
Of this last word we may note that the Septuagint renders it Μαγεδδω
Gesenius suggests that Megiddo may mean "a place of crowds."

Then immediately "the seventh vial is poured into the air," and the voice from heaven—from the temple, and from the throne—declares "IT IS DONE."[1] Now signs and wonders follow. Babylon receives her cup of wrath. The islands and the mountains flee away. And men's hearts failing them for fear, and their bodies suffering from the plague of hail, they blaspheme God.

Another subject of general inquiry, because thought to be of serious moment as a sign of the approach of Christ for judgment, is the PROPHESYING OF THE WITNESSES. On this also I have said nothing.

There can be no doubt that previous to the advent of our LORD, THE PROPHET ELIJAH will appear on earth.

That he has *not come yet*, is certain. JOHN THE BAPTIST was not ELIJAH. He *said* he was not. "I am *not* Elias," was his reply to those who asked him.[2] Our Lord indeed declared of him, "This is ELIAS *which was for to come*."[3] And so indeed *he was*. He was ELIAS as to "the *power* and *spirit*;"[4] the Elias (so to speak) who was to be the herald of the Saviour's *peaceful* mission. But he was *not* ELIAS—*in person*—not the *actual* ELIJAH who was taken up in the fiery chariot.

---

[1] See the position of the Seven Vials in *The Book of Revelation in Diagram*, by same author.

[2] John i. 21.   [3] Matt. ii. 14.   [4] Luke i. 17.

It was nowhere said he was to come before the *first—the peaceful*—day of the Lord Jesus;—but as MALACHI predicted—"before the coming of THE GREAT AND DREADFUL day of the Lord," the day when He shall come for judgment, and to take possession of His kingdom. No doubt, therefore, ELIJAH has *not yet appeared*, but IS TO COME. But where is the evidence that he is to be one of the "TWO WITNESSES?" We cannot find it. If we refer to the eleventh chapter of REVELATION, we shall see that the "TWO WITNESSES" are introduced, not under the *last*, but under the SIXTH trumpet. This trumpet *does not speak of* THE LORD'S ADVENT. It is the trumpet of the REFORMATION PERIOD.[1] It is *not* the trumpet which proclaims THE END.

I feel then no hesitation in asserting the opinion that the Two Witnesses, belonging as they do to this sixth trumpet, and not to that which proclaims the end of the dispensation, are none other than THE PROPHETS AND THE APOSTLES GENERALLY; or, in other words, THE OLD AND NEW TESTAMENT SCRIPTURES. But test this. It is certain that these inspired witnesses of God did prophesy, as it were, clothed in sackcloth for *twelve hundred and sixty years*; namely, from A.D. 533 (when the EDICT OF JUSTINIAN planted the nucleus of that persecuting power of the Papacy, which it swayed with

---

[1] Commencing probably at or about A.D. 1517.

such effect in after years) till the REIGN OF TERROR, 1793, when, so far as their existence in the Roman Empire was concerned, *they were slain;* and thus, for *three and a half years* (the time predicted) viz., from the 31st May, 1793 (at which time, by the success of the Jacobin Conspirators, the destruction of the civil establishment of religion in France was completed, the "Worship of Reason" commenced, the Scriptures were declared to be a fable, death was pronounced an everlasting sleep, the Sabbath was abolished, and the reckoning of time altered), to the beginning of the year 1797, (when a change took place by the fact of new men obtaining power in the great council of the Commonwealth.)

During this predicted period, it was as the prophecy declared it should be.[1] Joy was exhibited amongst the learned and scientific people of all Europe. They wrote one to another, offering congratulations on the introduction of a new era. Our own beloved country was infected also, and Republicanism and Infidelity committed ravages on every side.

But after the inspired witnesses had thus lain dead, unused, uncared for, scoffed at, despised, for the appointed period, "they *revived and stood upon their feet,*" and a day of greater honour dawned upon them than they ever, theretofore, experienced. They were read,

[1] Rev. xi. 10.

searched, believed, and propagated. Home and missionary effort sprang up,[1] and from *that* day to *this* there has been one continued call for praise and thanksgiving, because the Lord has glorified HIS WORD, and spread its voice of testimony throughout all the world, so that in every tongue its gospel message sounds, and every nation under heaven receives blessing through its heart-reviving witness. The PROPHETS and APOSTLES (as it were) "*ascended up to heaven,*" in the sight of their enemies. Indeed, all the details as laid down concerning these two witnesses in the eleventh chapter of the REVELATION, even to the earthquake, and the fall of the tenth part of the city,[2] were proved accurately true, as a mere glance at the history of the period will show clearly. Thus to my own mind there is satisfactory evidence that the *two witnesses* are to be looked for only in past history, though, thank God, in present and abiding power.

Having thus dealt with these two subjects (viz., Armageddon and the Witnesses), which are by so many

---

[1] It is worthy of note that the years 1799, 1804, and 1808 were marked respectively by the formation of the "Church Missionary," the "British and Foreign Bible," and the "London Jews" Societies.

[2] France, one of the ten parts of the Great Roman City, "the eldest son of the Roman Church," experienced a fall indeed at that fearful period of which we have been speaking, producing the most momentous effects of lasting character upon the whole of the old Roman Empire.

supposed to have immediate connexion with the Lord's Advent, let us again uplift our minds to those above— the SAINTS who have been called to meet the Lord in the air at the great Translation prior to the Tribulation.

According to the words of our Lord, recorded by MATTHEW and MARK, the angels are sent forth *after the last tribulation* to gather together the elect from one end of heaven to the other.[1] This will be a call, we may suppose, *to all the glorified ones who are above* to draw together in one grand assembly, because the looked-for time shall have arrived for the foretold descent upon the earth, that the great work of judgment may commence. In the nineteenth chapter of the REVELATION also a summons comes forth to those who are entitled "THE BRIDE," that they may be gathered to the "MARRIAGE SUPPER OF THE LAMB." These calls synchronize, and are probably identical. So we may conclude that the period between the entrance into heaven of the last saint from the earth's harvest[2] and the descent of the Redeemer to the Mount of Olives[3] is the time appointed for the celebration of this glorious festival.

Of the *nature* of the MARRIAGE SUPPER we are told *nothing*. It is only said, "Blessed are they which are

---

[1] Matt. xxiv. 31 ; Mark xiii. 27.
[2] Rev. xviii.   [3] Zech. xiv., and Rev. xiv. and xix.

called to the marriage supper of the Lamb." But now, the supper being ended, the heavens open, and the LORD, WITH ALL THE SHINING HOST OF THE REDEEMED, COMES FORTH. The inspired description, in allegory doubtless (though it *may* possess far less of what is allegorical than we imagine), is thus given—"And I saw heaven opened, and behold a white horse; and He that sat upon him was called Faithful and True, and in righteousness He doth judge and make war. His eyes were as a flame of fire, and on His head were many crowns; and He had a name written, that no man knew, but He Himself. And He was clothed with a vesture dipped in blood: and His name is called the WORD OF GOD. And the armies which were in heaven followed Him upon white horses, clothed in fine linen, white and clean (the righteousness of the saints). And out of His mouth goeth a sharp sword, that with it he should smite the nations; and He shall rule them with a rod of iron; and He treadeth the winepress of the fierceness and wrath of Almighty God. And He hath on His vesture and on His thigh a name written, "KING OF KINGS AND LORD OF LORDS."[1]

Thus, whatever the details of this allegory may in themselves signify, we find our Lord (THE WORD OF GOD, THE KING OF KINGS, THE LORD OF LORDS) accom-

---

[1] See Rev. xix.

panied by all the multitude of His redeemed saints, issuing forth in awful majesty and power from the high place above, where, through the period of the last great tribulation, He had kept His people in security.

But for a moment we must look again at earth. "THE SIGN OF THE SON OF MAN" has appeared in heaven, in the sight of the wicked world. "The sign" (το σημειον), some evidence, some clear intimation, which men cannot gainsay. *It appears*, and "the tribes of the earth mourn."[1] The heaven departs "as a scroll when it is rolled together," and reveals the wondrous truth. THE DESPISED JESUS AND HIS ONCE PERSECUTED PEOPLE ARE DESCENDING. "Every mountain and island are moved out of their places. And the kings of the earth, and the great men, and the rich men, and the chief captains, and the mighty men, and every bondman, and every freeman, hide themselves in the dens and in the rocks of the mountains; and say to the mountains and rocks, Fall on us, and hide us from the face of Him that sitteth on the throne, and from the wrath of the Lamb; for the great day of His wrath is come, and who shall be able to stand?"[2] But He descends. "*This same Jesus who was seen to go into heaven, so descends in like manner as He was seen to go into heaven.*"[3] And, as ZECHARIAH tells us, He stands upon the Mount of Olives, and the

[1] Matt. xxiv. 30.   [2] Rev. vi. 14–17.   [3] Acts i. 2.

mountain cleaves in the midst thereof towards the east
and towards the west: and half of the mountain removes
towards the north, and half of it towards the south.[1]

Standing on that very Mount of Olives, where in
time gone by He rode meekly on an ass's colt, THE KING
OF KINGS SHALL MANIFEST HIMSELF in glory, and
the opened heaven shall reveal His hosts in multitudes
beyond the power of number. The sun shall become
dark; the moon and stars refuse their light; the glory of
the Lord of heaven shall strike terror through the length
and breadth of earth, and "every eye shall see Him." The
vision of His dreadful majesty no man shall be permitted to escape; but as "the lightning coming from the
east shineth even unto the west," so shall be the glory
of the Lord's descent.[2] As the bright shining of the
lights of heaven is beheld *by all*, so will be the coming
of the Son of God. All will see it. No man will escape
it. That fearful glory—that ineffable greatness—THE
MAJESTY OF THE KING OF KINGS, THE JUDGE, THE
GOD, THE MAN, THE EXPRESS IMAGE OF THE HEAVENLY
FATHER'S PERSON—shall not be escaped nor hidden from
the view of any soul on earth. "BEHOLD HE COMETH
WITH CLOUDS; AND EVERY EYE SHALL SEE HIM, AND
THEY ALSO WHO PIERCED HIM; AND ALL KINDREDS OF
THE EARTH SHALL WAIL BECAUSE OF HIM."

[1] Zech. xiv. 4.   [2] Matt. xxiv. 57.

Such will be the introduction of THE GREAT DAY OF JUDGMENT. The day of such unspeakable delight to an innumerable multitude; but of terror beyond all description to the workers of iniquity.

When that GREAT DAY shall dawn, WILL ALL BE WELL WITH US? Let no one put this question from him; it is far too serious to be deferred. If we would have it to be well with us in *that* day, we must see that it is well in *this.* "*Now* is the day of salvation." Happy those (and why should not this be the estate of *all?*) who can look up with confidence, and find, in the great King and Judge, a Friend! O that it were graven on the heart of every sinner while this day of grace endures—while yet His coming lingers—while yet His "sign" appears not in the vault of heaven—that THE ALMIGHTY JESUS IS THE SYMPATHIZING FRIEND OF EVERY SIN-BOUND SOUL! Is there not *love,* is there not *pity,* is there not the *tenderest sympathy,* in those once pierced hands and feet—in that agonized frame—that blood—that heavenward cry? Is there not compassion in that Seat of Mediation on which One who is A MAN, OUR BROTHER, sits? Is there not constraining grace in those most precious words of Jesus, "WHOSOEVER LIVETH AND BELEVETH IN ME, SHALL NEVER DIE."[1]

[1] John xi. 26.

CHAPTER V.

The Judgment of the Nations.

"In righteousness He doth judge and make war."—REV. xix. 11.

RELIGIOUS people often speak of "THE LAST DAY,"
—"THE DAY OF THE LORD,"—or "THE DAY
OF JUDGMENT;" as if it were to be a day of
ordinary duration, to come suddenly upon the world: a
certain day of twelve or four-and-twenty hours, appointed
by the Father, in which a complete destruction of all
sublunary, if not heavenly, things is to take place; and
the righteous and the wicked being raised and judged,
rewards and punishments of everlasting nature are to be
awarded them.[1]

This is perfectly correct so far as may concern the
great events which shall transpire. "The day of the
Lord"—the Apostle PETER tells us—"will come as a
thief in the night; in which the heavens will pass away
with a great noise, and the elements shall melt with

[1] Introductory Chapter.

fervent heat; the earth, also, and the works that are therein, shall be burned up."[1] Moreover, as OUR LORD Himself has told us—"When the Son of man shall come in His glory, and all the holy angels with Him, then shall He sit upon the throne of His glory; and before Him shall be gathered all nations; and He shall separate them one from another, as a shepherd divideth his sheep from the goats, and He shall set the sheep on His right hand, but the goats on the left." And those on His left hand "shall go away into everlasting punishment, but the righteous into life eternal."[2]

So far, therefore, as the events spoken of in the popular tradition are themselves concerned, there is correctness which cannot be gainsayed. But there seems to be decided *incorrectness* therein, as to the PERIOD OF ENDURANCE which has been assigned to "the Great Day," and also as to the ORDER in which the events of that day will transpire as it passes onward from its morning to its evening.

The word "DAY" is often used in Holy Scripture to signify a certain period of time, marked out distinctly from all other periods, but not necessarily of either *this* or *that* precise duration. So, we remember, CHRIST very plainly used the word, saying—"Your Father Abraham rejoiced to see *My day*; and he saw it, and

---

[1] 2 Pet. iii. 10.　　　　[2] Matt. xxv. 31.

was glad."[1] Thus; too, the Apostle PAUL—"The *night* is far spent, the *day* is at hand."[2] And the same elsewhere. For our present purpose, however, the words of Peter are most suitable in the third chapter of his Second Epistle, where it is written—"The heavens and the earth which are now, by the same word are kept in store, reserved unto fire against THE DAY OF JUDGMENT AND PERDITION OF UNGODLY MEN. But, beloved, be not ignorant of this one thing, that ONE DAY IS WITH THE LORD AS A THOUSAND YEARS, AND A THOUSAND YEARS AS ONE DAY."

But what does the Apostle mean? Can it be that he would afford a hint, as it were, *that the Great Day of Judgment will endure* ONE THOUSAND YEARS? or does he refer only to the period to which the Lord may possibly *delay* His coming,—and seek to found thereon an argument on the behalf of patient waiting till He shall appear? The latter certainly is the more probable. But, judging from what is said in other parts of Scripture, we may think it *possible* that *both* these lessons were intended to be given.

We will at any rate *suppose* it so to be, and dwell awhile upon the *former* of the two, that we may see if anything is clearly placed before us in the Bible which will lead to the conclusion that the day of judgment

John viii. 56.   [2] Rom. xiii. 12.

will endure *a thousand years*, or any lengthened period which in the prophetic language *might be so expressed.*[1]

We have seen that the Lord will come, and in a fearful stroke of judgment sweep, as with a besom of destruction, the rebellious people from the surface of the world; that in the Valley of Jehoshaphat,—the Valley of Decision,—He will judge the nations with a just but heavy stroke. This Act of Judgment will introduce the MORNING of the Last Great Day,— "The Day of God Almighty."

But the morning of the day will pass, and brighter hours succeed. The nations shall rejoice and sing for joy, because the Lord shall judge them righteously. The people shall all praise Him. The earth shall yield her increase, and God shall give mankind His blessing.[2] Thus shall the MERIDIAN of "that day" be occupied. And now again,—Another scene, a scene of wonder, terrible in its display, and fearful, yet most blessed, in its grand result, shall be enacted. The Great King will sit upon the throne of His glory, and every

---

[1] "The sentiments of the learned, humble, and pious MEDE will have weight with those who really know his writings. He remarks, ... I do not indeed think we are to expect two Advents of Christ; but one, namely, that in which He will judge the quick and the dead at His appearing; but that both His Advent and His Judgment will be protracted through the period of a thousand years."

Bickersteth's Guide to the Prophecies, p. 248.

[2] Psalm lxvii. 3-5.

soul which has in any age existed on the surface of the
earth, shall stand before Him. Then shall every secret
be revealed, and every hidden thought be made manifest.
Then shall the unerring JUDGMENT OF MANKIND be set,
and the Eternal Record-books be opened. Then shall
the heavens pass away, the elements dissolve, the earth
and all therein be burned with fire. Then shall sin
come to an everlasting end, and Death itself be cast into
the appointed Lake. Thus shall the EVENING of "that
day" be passed, and all things be prepared for an
eternal state, where times and seasons are not to be
known, but one unbroken day of unalloyed delight is to
pursue its course through a most glorious age, the length
of which infinity alone can measure.

So, as there was, first, a PATRIARCHAL DAY; then, a
DAY OF TYPES AND SHADOWS under the Mosaic Ritual;
and after that a DAY OF CHRISTIAN DISPENSATION;
there will be yet one other DAY—"THE DAY OF THE
LORD," "THE DAY OF JUDGMENT," "THE LAST DAY;"
after which will be ETERNITY.

The present chapter will be occupied with the consideration of those great events which will peculiarly
mark the MORNING of this "Last Day." I have
included these events, when mentioning "the general
order" of our subjects, under the title of "THE JUDGMENT
OF THE NATIONS," in the Introductory Chapter.

The terms in which the PROPHETS speak of this Judgment of the Nations is exceedingly impressive. Their language points to it as one of the greatest among great events. The world is represented as being full of wickedness; the hand of cruelty uplifted high; the thoughts of all men far from Him in whose hand is their life, their breath, and all things. But suddenly a check is laid upon their rashness. The Lord descends. He comes with all His Saints, who, as we have seen,[1] have been caught up at the first blast of the last trumpet to meet Him in the air, and so are ready to descend with Him. He comes in righteousness to judge and make war: He comes prepared to avenge the blood of all His servants who have fallen by the hand of wickedness: He comes in readiness to vindicate His honour in the sight of the ungodly, and to take possession of the throne which appertains to Him as "KING OF KINGS and LORD OF LORDS."

ISAIAH tells us, in his second chapter, that "it shall come to pass in the last days, that the mountain of the Lord's house shall be established in the top of the mountains, and shall be exalted above the hills; and all nations shall flow into it. And many people shall go and say, Come ye, and let us go up to the mountain of the Lord, to the house of the God of Jacob:

---

[1] See page 104.

and He will teach us of His ways, and we will walk in
His paths: for out of Zion shall go forth the law, and
the word of the Lord from Jerusalem." The prophet
thus foretels a very glorious time: a time yet future,
such as has not hitherto appeared. But more is added,
marking definitely the period thus referred to. "And
they shall beat their swords into ploughshares, and their
spears into pruning-hooks; nation shall not lift up sword
against nation, neither shall they learn war any more."
Referring to the former part of the *third verse,* we see
by what this period of unprecedented peace will be
introduced. "AND HE (THE LORD) SHALL JUDGE AMONG
THE NATIONS, AND REBUKE MANY PEOPLE." Thus, *before
the millennial glory shall dawn upon the world,* the Lord
shall institute an act of judgment. "He shall judge
among the nations, and rebuke many people; and they
shall beat their swords into ploughshares." The ACT
OF JUDGMENT *first,* and the STATE OF PEACE AND
RIGHTEOUSNESS *afterwards.* But a little further down
the chapter we have *minute information* given us concerning this great introductory act of judgment. "Enter
into the rock, and hide thee in the dust, for fear of the
Lord, and for the glory of His majesty. The lofty looks
of man shall be humbled, and the haughtiness of men
shall be bowed down, and the Lord alone shall be
exalted in that day. For the day of the Lord of hosts

shall be upon every one that is proud and lofty, and upon every one that is lifted up, and he shall be brought low. And the loftiness of man shall be bowed down, and the haughtiness of men shall be made low; and the Lord alone shall be exalted in that day. And the idols he shall utterly abolish. And they shall go into the holes of the rocks, and into the caves of the earth, for fear of the Lord, and for the glory of His majesty, when He ariseth to shake terribly the earth." Again, in the *fourth chapter*—"And it shall come to pass that he that is left in Zion, and he that remaineth in Jerusalem, shall be called holy, even *every one that is written among the living in Jerusalem;* when the Lord shall have washed away the filth of the daughters of Zion, and shall have purged away the blood of Jerusalem from the midst thereof, *by the spirit of judgment and by the spirit of burning.*" Or the *twenty-fourth chapter.* The latter part of this chapter speaks of a fearful period of trouble which shall come to pass as the end approaches; a period to which we have referred at length in the Second Chapter of this work.

The prophet having foretold the *final tribulation* in language which leaves not the slightest room for doubt concerning its severity, tells us of *the earth* [1]

---

[1] I suppose "the earth" in this place to mean, not the whole world but *the land* of Israel. Compare Zech. xiv. 4, and 10.

reeling to and fro like a drunkard, and being removed like a cottage by reason of the heavy transgression which shall be upon it, and forewarns us of an act of judgment which shall mark that day; not as to its general progress from the morning till the evening, but its *introduction only*. This is evident, for he declares that *after* the great act of judgment shall be ended, the reign of the Lord of hosts in Jerusalem shall commence. "And it shall come to pass in that day, that the Lord shall punish the host of the high ones that are on high, and the kings of the earth upon the earth. And they shall be gathered together, as prisoners are gathered in the pit, and shall be shut up in the prison, and after many days they shall be visited. Then the moon shall be confounded, and the sun ashamed, when the Lord of hosts shall reign in Mount Zion, and in Jerusalem, and before His ancients gloriously." This is surely plain. There is to be *an act of fearful judgment* against the wicked nations and their rulers, *introductory* to the Lord of hosts assuming the millennial throne in Zion. For we find that "the host of the high ones that are on high," the unconverted people of the world, probably, who serve the prince of the power of the air,[1] and show allegiance to wicked spirits in high or heavenly places,[2] will be visited with summary punishment. They are to

---

[1] Eph. ii. 2.   [2] Eph. vi. 12.

be gathered together as prisoners are gathered in the pit, and to be shut up in prison, and there kept "many days." *Many days only. Not for ever.* For a day will come when they must "*be visited*" and brought before the throne of judgment, to receive, with all the world besides, an everlasting sentence, in accordance with their deeds.

JOEL speaks very plainly on the subject. In the third chapter—to which reference has been made [1] with regard to the gathering of all nations against Jerusalem, we read—"Behold, in those days, when I bring again the captivity of Judah and Jerusalem, I will also gather all nations, and will bring them down to the valley of Jehoshaphat, and will plead with them there. . . . . Let the heathen come up to the valley of Jehoshaphat, *for there will I sit to judge all the heathen round about.* . . . . Multitudes, multitudes in the Valley of Decision; for the DAY OF THE LORD is near, in the Valley of Decision. The sun and the moon shall be darkened, and the stars shall withdraw their shining." Surely, so far as this passage affords information, "he may run that readeth" what God will do when He shall appear on the behalf of Israel. He will "*plead with*"—He will "*judge*"— the nations. The *valley of Jehoshaphat* will be the place of judgment; there He will sit and execute the fierceness

[1] Chap. iv.

of His anger, while the sun and the moon shall become dark, and the stars shall withdraw their shining. Now this act of judgment will be preparatory to the establishment of Israel in the full possession of their land; for we are told—immediately after this declaration of judgment and terror is made—that " the Lord also shall roar out of ZION, and utter His voice from JERUSALEM; and the heavens and the earth shall shake; but the Lord will be the hope of His people, and the strength of the children of Israel. So shall ye know that I am the Lord your God, dwelling in Zion, My holy mountain: then shall Jerusalem be holy, and there shall no strangers pass through her any more. And it shall come to pass in that day, that the mountains shall drop down new wine, and the hills shall flow with milk, and ... Judah shall dwell for ever, and Jerusalem from generation to generation. For I will cleanse their blood that I have not cleansed: for the Lord dwelleth in Zion." How evident it is, then, that the great act of judgment upon the nations shall *precede and immediately introduce* the happy reign of Israel's peace!

Let us hear another prophet. By ZEPHANIAH, in the third chapter, we find the Lord speaking thus: " My determination is to gather the nations, that I may assemble the KINGDOMS, to pour upon them Mine indignation, even all My fierce anger; for all the earth shall be devoured by the fire of My jealousy." And now let us mark what follows—"Then will I return to the people a pure language, that they may all call upon the name of the Lord, to serve Him with one consent. . . . . The remnant of Israel shall do no iniquity, nor speak lies; neither shall a deceitful tongue be found in their mouth: for they shall feed, and lie down, and none shall make them afraid. . . . . The King of Israel, even the Lord, is in the midst of thee: thou shalt not see evil any more." Here, then, again the same lesson is advanced.

And so likewise does the Prophet ZECHARIAH speak. The tenth, eleventh, twelfth, and thirteenth chapters speak of ISRAEL *first* RESTORED IN UNBELIEF under the auspices of "THE IDOL SHEPHERD;" *then* BESIEGED BY ALL NATIONS; and *at last* DRIVEN TO A BITTER MOURNING FOR THEIR SINS, AND A TRUE-HEARTED RETURN TO GOD IN CHRIST. The fourteenth chapter retraces a little, and gives valuable explanation. It says—"Behold, the day of the Lord cometh, and thy spoil shall be divided in the midst of thee. For I will gather all nations against Jerusalem to battle; and the city shall be taken, and the houses rifled, and the women ravished; and half of the city shall go forth into captivity, and the residue of the people shall not be cut off from the city." This will be the sign of the immediate Advent, for it is added, "THEN SHALL THE LORD GO FORTH, and fight against those nations, as when He fought in the day of battle. And His feet shall stand in that day upon the Mount of Olives, which is before Jerusalem on the east; and the Mount of Olives shall cleave in the midst thereof, towards the east and towards the west, and there shall be a very great valley; and half of the mountain shall remove toward the north, and half of it toward the south. And ye shall flee to the valley of the mountain; for the valley of the mountains shall reach unto Azal; yea, ye shall flee, like as ye fled from before the earthquake in the days of Uzziah, king of Judah: AND THE LORD MY GOD SHALL COME, AND ALL THE SAINTS WITH THEE, . . . and the Lord shall be King over all the earth, ... and there shall be no more utter destruction; but Jerusalem shall be safely inhabited."

So, then, we are left without a doubt, that when the Lord shall come again upon our earth, it will be to perform *at once* an act of FEARFUL JUDGMENT ON THE NATIONS. And we are prepared to understand the declaration in the nineteenth chapter of the REVELATION, where the descent of Him who bears the title "King of kings and Lord of lords" is spoken of—"And I saw an angel standing in the sun: and he cried with a loud voice, saying to all the fowls that fly in the midst of heaven, Come and gather yourselves together to the supper of the great God : that ye may eat the flesh of kings, and the flesh of captains, and the flesh of mighty men, and the flesh of horses, and of them that sit on them, and the flesh of all men, both free and bond, both small and great."

But while we speak of the Lord's judgment of the wicked nations, we must not omit to notice the peculiar stress which is laid, both in the OLD and NEW Testaments, upon the heavy stroke of judgment which shall fall on HIM who shall have been THE LEADER, first of ISRAEL to the re-possession of their land, and then of ALL THE NATIONS of the earth, in siege against their tribes.

In the tenth chapter of ISAIAH we read of "THE ASSYRIAN :"—probably the ancient dynasty of Assyrian monarchs and their works of power, as God's instrument for the punishment of Israel. But in the *twelfth verse* we find the following prediction :—" It shall come to pass, that, when the Lord hath performed His WHOLE WORK upon Mount Zion and on Jerusalem, I will punish THE FRUIT of the stout heart of the King of Assyria, and the glory of his looks. For he saith, By the strength of my hand have I done it, and by my wisdom ; for I am prudent ; and I have removed the bounds of the people, and have robbed their treasures, and I have put down the inhabitants like a valiant man; and my hand hath found, as a nest, the riches of the people. . . . . O my people, that dwellest in Zion, be not afraid of the Assyrian; . . . . for yet a very little while and the indignation shall cease, and Mine anger in their destruction. And the Lord of Hosts shall stir up a scourge for him, according to the slaughter of Midian at the rock of Oreb. . . . . And it shall come to pass in that day, that his burden shall be taken from off thy shoulder, and his yoke from off thy neck, and the yoke shall be destroyed, because of the anointing. . . . . He shall shake his hand against the Mount of the daughter of Zion, the Hill of Jerusalem. Behold, the Lord, *the Lord of Hosts, shall lop the bough with terror*, and the high ones of stature shall be hewn down, and the haughty ones shall be humbled." And immediately upon this prophecy of the Assyrian's destruction, the "ROD OUT OF THE STEM OF JESSE" is brought before us, and the reign of righteousness and peace is introduced. Again, in the *fourteenth chapter*, the prophet gives us an account of the events which shall take place at the destruction of the mysterious Babylon of the latter days, and tells us that the last king thereof—"THE ASSYRIAN"—shall meet with his END IN THE LAND OF ISRAEL. "I will break the Assyrian (saith the Lord) *in My land, and upon My mountains.*"

In DANIEL (the eleventh chapter, in which the same LAST KING OF THE LAST EMPIRE is evidently spoken of[1]), we read that "He shall plant the tabernacles of his palace between the seas in the glorious holy mountain; yet he shall come to his end, and none shall help him. And at that time shall Michael stand up: the great prince which standeth for the children of thy people."

The same fact is implied in the language of the Apostle PAUL, where he declares—that *the Lord will consume that wicked one with the spirit of His mouth, and destroy him with the brightness of His coming.*[2] For this is tantamount to saying that *at* or *near* the very place where Jesus Christ shall appear (namely, in the land of Israel), the stroke of judgment will descend upon the head of Antichrist.

So, then, upon the repeated word of Scripture, we conclude that ANTICHRIST WILL RECEIVE HIS PORTION OF THE LORD'S FIRST ACT OF JUDGMENT, AND THAT HE WILL RECEIVE IT IN THE LAND OF ISRAEL.

But these passages and others show us likewise *what the express judgment shall be* which this WICKED ONE shall receive.

In the fourteenth chapter of ISAIAH, we find that he shall "be cut down to the ground, . . . brought down to the grave, ... TO HELL, TO THE SIDES OF THE PIT,

[1] Chapter III.   [2] 2 Thess. ii. 8.

L

cast out of the grave like an abominable branch. In the *thirtieth chapter*, which speaks of the same terminal period and the same events which are elsewhere brought forward as the characteristic marks of "the last time," we find the Prophet speaking thus—"The Lord shall cause His glorious voice to be heard, and shall show the lighting down of His arm, with the indignation of His anger, and with the flame of a devouring fire, with scattering, and tempest, and hailstones. For through the voice of the Lord shall the ASSYRIAN be beaten down, which smote with a rod. For TOPHET is ordained of old; yea, for the KING it is prepared: He hath made it deep and large; the pile thereof is fire and much wood: the breath of the Lord, like a stream of brimstone, doth kindle it."

Thus the judgment of "the Assyrian" will be a judgment of severity. He will be "brought down to hell," being beaten down by "the voice of the Lord," and he will be consigned to the fire of Tophet.

DANIEL speaks very clearly with reference to the manner in which the FOURTH (or Roman) EMPIRE shall be overthrown; but of "THE LITTLE HORN"—THE ANTI-CHRIST—which arises out of that Empire, the *bare fact* of his destruction is *all* that we find related. Of the EMPIRE it is said—"I beheld even till the beast was slain, and his body destroyed, and given to the burning flame." [1] But of the HORN, the last king thereof—the Antichrist—it is said,—"He shall be broken without hand." [2] The wrath "determined shall be poured upon him." [3] "He shall come to his end and none shall help him." [4]

We have referred already to the word of the Apostle PAUL upon the subject: "Then shall that WICKED be revealed, whom the Lord shall consume with the spirit of His mouth, and destroy with the brightness of His coming." [5] But let us observe how closely this agrees with that which was advanced by ISAIAH and DANIEL. The "voice" of the Lord,—"the breath of the Lord like a stream of brimstone,"—"the spirit of His mouth," —is the instrument; and the destruction takes place "without hand,"—"with the flame of a devouring fire," —"with the brightness of His coming."

Let us make one more reference. In the nineteenth chapter of the REVELATION (which speaks particularly of the Advent of our Lord with His Saints) we find the Apostle John declaring,—"I saw the beast, and the kings of the earth, and their armies, gathered together to make war against Him that sat upon the horse (that is, "the King of kings"), and against His army. And the BEAST was taken, and with him the FALSE PROPHET,

---

[1] Dan. vii. 11.   [2] Dan. viii. 25.   [3] Dan. ix. 27.
[4] Dan. xi. 45.   [5] 2 Thess. ii. 8.

that wrought miracles before him, with which he deceived them that had received the mark of the beast,
and them that worshipped his image. THESE BOTH
WERE CAST ALIVE INTO A LAKE OF FIRE, BURNING WITH
BRIMSTONE. And the remnant were slain with the
sword of Him that sat upon the horse, which sword
proceeded out of His mouth."

This is the most detailed account of Antichrist's
destruction which is given us. And here we find
again entire agreement with the assertions which have
preceded.

So then, *in the Holy Land, at the Advent of the Lord,
by the breath of His mouth, with the brightness of His
coming,* SHALL ANTICHRIST MEET HIS DESTRUCTION. He
shall be taken *with the False Prophet,* and be cast alive
into *the lake of fire*—the *"Tophet"* which was ordained
of old and prepared *"for the king."* Thus shall these
two workers of iniquity have their portion in the lake
of fire and brimstone, before others, *even before Satan
himself;* for the twentieth chapter of REVELATION
teaches us that Satan will abide for yet a thousand years
before he shall be cast into this lake, because there is
a final stroke of wickedness which he must be reserved
to execute, to the great end that sin may be *for ever*
overthrown. And then it is declared, "the devil that
deceiveth" the nations shall be "cast into the lake of

fire and brimstone, where the beast and the false prophet are, and shall be tormented day and night for ever and ever." But of this we have to speak hereafter.

We have mentioned "THE FALSE PROPHET," as the companion of the Antichrist. His bosom friend, it would appear: his counsellor, his priest; the one by whom he is to work his miracles. Expounders of Prophecy have varied much in their ideas respecting this person. Some have spoken of him very confidently as the last Bishop of Rome, but having his seat transferred to *Jerusalem*, and there, taking part with Antichrist in denying both the Father and the Son,[1] and in establishing idolatry. Others, that he will be some individual holding, or pretending to hold, an intimate communication with spiritual existences. Others, again, have held notions of a kind very different from these; considering him, as they consider Antichrist, to be either *an apostate Church*, or an *infidel system*, having great pretensions.

It will be readily conceived, from the general tone of this work, that I believe the FALSE PROPHET will be a PERSON. But whether he will have an episcopal or papal title, or whether he will be an infidel necromancer, I do not find so far revealed, that any fair hypothesis can be laid down about the matter. The day of Antichrist will show the world quite soon enough concerning such a wicked one.

[1] 1 John ii. 22.

When these great powers of evil shall have been consigned to their own place, and the remnant of the workers of iniquity shall have been "slain with the sword of Him that sitteth upon the horse,"[1] the world will have assumed a fearful aspect. But few men, by comparison, will be left, while multitudes from all nations will be slain. "There shall be as the shaking of an olive tree, and as the gleaning grapes when the vintage is done:"[2] a remnant left to *Israel*, and a seed among the Gentiles. That such a remnant *will* be left is evident, for the Word of God has plainly declared it.

ISAIAH, in the tenth chapter, where he speaks, as we have shown already, of the destruction of Antichrist and the ungodly nations, says—"Therefore shall the Lord, the Lord of Hosts, send among His fat ones leanness; and under His glory He shall kindle a burning, like the burning of a fire, ... and it shall consume the glory of His forest, and of His fruitful field, *both soul and body :* and they shall be as when a standard-bearer fainteth. *And the rest of the trees of the forest shall be few, that a child may write them.* And it shall come to pass in that day that the REMNANT OF ISRAEL, and such as are escaped of the House of Judah, shall stay upon the Lord, the Holy One of Israel, in truth. *The remnant shall return, even the remnant of Jacob, unto the mighty God.*"

---

[1] Rev. xix. 21.   [2] Isa. xxiv.

JEREMIAH also, in his thirtieth chapter, speaks by
the Word of God to Israel—"Though I make a full
end of all nations whither I have scattered thee, *yet will
I not make a full end of thee :* but I will correct thee in
measure, and will not leave thee altogether unpunished."

JOEL foretels plainly, in the second chapter, of the
remnant which shall be spared in the last day, thus :—
"It shall come to pass, that whosoever shall call on the
name of the Lord shall be delivered : for in Mount Zion
and in Jerusalem shall be deliverance, as the Lord hath
said, and in the remnant whom the Lord shall call."

ZECHARIAH, in the thirteenth chapter, speaking in
the name of the Lord, says—"I will bring *the third part*
through the fire, and will refine them as silver is refined,
and will try them as gold is tried; they shall call on
My name, and I will hear them; I will say, It is My
people; and they shall say, The Lord is my God."

Of the Remnant of *Israel* which is chiefly brought
before us in these passages, we are taught by JEREMIAH
and ZECHARIAH,[1] that they shall be brought to the Lord
"with weeping and with supplications." That God
"will pour upon the house of David and the inhabitants
of Jerusalem the spirit of grace and of supplications;"
and they shall look on "Him whom they have pierced,
and they shall mourn for Him, as one mourneth for his

[1] Jer. xxxi. 8–25 ; Zech. xii. 10–14.

only son, and shall be in bitterness for Him, as one that
is in bitterness for his first-born." Thus, therefore, *at
the eleventh hour*, there shall be mercy for the remnant
of Israel, " according to the election of grace."

But also, there shall be, as we have said, a remnant
from among the *Gentile* nations ; for the Ensign will be
upreared for *them :* as it is written in the eleventh
chapter of ISAIAH—"And in that day (the day of the
Redeemer's reign of peace) there shall be a root of
Jesse, which shall stand up for an ensign *of the people ;*
to it shall the *Gentiles* seek; and His rest shall be
glorious." So again, in the *sixtieth chapter*, we read,
"The *Gentiles* shall come to thy (Israel's) light, and
kings to the brightness of thy rising, ... the forces of
the *Gentiles* shall come unto thee, ... surely the isles
shall wait for me, and the ships of Tarshish first, to
bring thy sons from far, ... unto the name of the
Lord thy God, and to the Holy One of Israel, because
He hath glorified thee. And the sons of strangers shall
build up thy walls, and their kings shall minister unto
thee. . . . The *sons* also of them that afflicted thee shall
come bending unto thee : and all that despised thee
shall bow themselves down at the soles of thy feet ; and
they shall call thee, the city of the Lord, the Zion of
the Holy One of Israel." But how shall this be, unless
a remnant of the Gentile nations shall be left ? Doubt-

less, both of JEWS and GENTILES there will be many who *knew not* the Lord's will, for lack of opportunity; many *afar off, who have never heard Christ's fame nor seen His glory :* many to whom His word has been a sealed book; a multitude, moreover, there will be of those whose *tender years of infancy* will hold them free from meriting the scourge of judgment when rebel nations meet their doom.

THUS WILL MEN BE GATHERED TO REPEOPLE THE EARTH, AND BOW SUBMISSIVELY BENEATH THE RIGHTEOUS SCEPTRE OF THE KING OF KINGS.

So far, we have looked upon the work of the *first act* of judgment which is to fall upon the ranks of men. It remains now only that we note the *last* important deed which is to mark the morning of the Lord's Great Day—THE PUNISHMENT OF SATAN.

This ARCH-DECEIVER, as we have already seen, is not yet to be consigned to the *eternal fire.* His work is not yet done.

The *twentieth chapter* of the REVELATION commences thus :—" And I saw an angel come down from heaven, having the key of the bottomless pit, and a great chain in his hand. And he laid hold on the DRAGON, that OLD SERPENT, which is the DEVIL and SATAN; and BOUND HIM A THOUSAND YEARS, and cast him into the BOTTOMLESS PIT, and shut him up, and set a seal upon him, that he should deceive the nations no more, *till the thousand years shall be fulfilled.*

With such words we must be content. Explain we *cannot.* We dare not say that this is allegory. But be that as it may, the lesson it conveys is clear. The power of Satan will be taken from him, so that he will tempt mankind no longer for a season. He will no more walk as a roaring lion, to and fro, seeking whom he may devour. The trembling babe in Christ will have no longer need to fear because of him. No saint will be accused by him before the throne of God. He will be powerless towards mankind for the long period of " A THOUSAND YEARS."

So will the MORNING of the DAY OF CHRIST—the DAY OF JUDGMENT—terminate. Oh, what a morning will it be! What man can picture it? A morn replete with what is fearful for the child of this world—glorious as the dawn of a bright day of joy unprecedented for the child of grace. O blessed thought! The *weakest among those who now look up with faith to Jesus,*[1] shall be delivered out of all the fear and woe which shall be poured down from heaven. He shall *behold* it all. The

---

[1] Yes, "The weakest;" for "Whosoever believeth that Jesus is the Christ is born of God" (1 John v. 1), and is Baptized by the Spirit into the Body of Christ (1 Cor. xii. 12, 13) ; and so is a very member of Christ, and without him Christ's fulness (Ephes. i. 23) would not be made up.

reeling earth, the raging sea, the madness of the people, he shall look upon, but in perfect peace. He shall hear the wicked call upon the rocks to fall upon them, and the hills to cover them; he shall observe the wonders which shall make the heavens shake, but with a mind unruffled and devoid of fear; for with the rejoicing hosts of Jesus shall his place be found: amidst the shining throng which shall adorn the triumph of the Lord shall be his rest. With Christ, the King, he shall descend from the high places of the saint's security. He shall descend not to endure the bitter stroke of judgment, but to *judge;* to sit with the great LORD OF LORDS upon the throne of the Millennial kingdom; to be a KING, A PRIEST, A CO-HEIR WITH THE PRINCE OF PEACE AND GLORY, IN POSSESSION OF THE HEIRDOM.

Reader, IS IT WELL WITH YOU, that so you will not fail of safety in the awful ADVENT HOUR? That hour with which the dreadful morning of the JUDGMENT DAY shall dawn? Surely this is not a matter for delay. "*Now* is the accepted time." *To-morrow* may not be. Oh, then suffer the plain question, ARE YOU NOW IN CHRIST? Have you yet gone to Him, *as a poor, helpless, worthless sinner,* and cast all your burden on His love and power to save? WHERE ARE YOUR SINS? Have you realized the fact that JESUS CHRIST has borne the utmost sin of *every believer* in His own body on the tree

—has suffered their full penalty—has washed their guilt away with infinitely precious blood—has made atonement for them, full, perfect, and eternal? Have you trusted His completed work for pardon and salvation? Surely it is written in the unchanging records of His tender mercy, "WHOSOEVER LIVETH AND BELIEVETH IN ME SHALL NEVER DIE."

CHAPTER VI.

The Reign of Peace.

"Behold, a King shall reign in righteousness, and princes shall rule in
judgment."—ISA. xxxii. 1.

WE have now to look upon the tribulation of the
latter days as *past*—the dominance of Iniquity,
Bloodshed, and Perplexity at an end—Antichrist consigned to the eternal flames—the wicked of
the earth destroyed—the Remnant brought to the ac-
knowledgment of Christ as Lord and Saviour—Satan
no longer able to deceive—and, visibly among mankind
and angels, the self-same JESUS who was crucified,
standing on the Mount of Olives, unopposed by any voice
throughout the earth, and there establishing His right
to reign as King of kings and Lord of lords. So will
the Almighty God fulfil His ancient word, which said
—"And thou, profane, wicked prince of Israel, whose
day is come, when iniquity shall have an end, Thus
saith the Lord God: Remove the diadem, and take off
the crown; this shall not be the same: exalt him that

is low, and abase him that is high. I will overturn,
overturn, overturn it; and it shall be no more, until
He come *whose right it is;* and I will give it Him."[1]
And thus the kingdom of the Lord of Hosts will come,
—wherein His holy will shall be performed in earth
as it is done in heaven.

This REIGN OF CHRIST—the reign of RIGHTEOUSNESS
and PEACE—will form the subject of this chapter.

Among the remnant of Israel—some inhabiting the
Holy Land, and some dispersed among the nations—
will be found a company from EVERY TRIBE: for God
has promised that "He will be the God of *all* the families
of Israel."[2] And so not only will MOUNT ZION rejoice,
but MOUNT EPHRAIM also, as the Lord graciously
declared by JEREMIAH in the thirty-first chapter of his
prophecy—"Behold I will bring them from the north
country, and gather them from the coasts of the earth,
. . . . a great company shall return thither. They
shall come with weeping, and with supplications will
I lead them: I will cause them to walk by the rivers
of waters in a straight way, wherein they shall not
stumble; for I am a Father to ISRAEL and EPHRAIM
is my first-born. Hear ye the Word of the Lord, O
ye nations, and declare it in the isles afar off, and say,
He that scattereth ISRAEL will gather him, and keep

---

[1] Ezek. xxi. 25-27. [2] Jer. xxxi. 1.

him as a shepherd doth his flock. . . . . Behold the days come, saith the Lord, that I will make a New Covenant *with the house of* ISRAEL *and with the house of* JUDAH."

So, too, did EZEKIEL prophesy in the thirty-seventh chapter. God had told him to take *two* sticks, and to "join them one to another into one stick," and when the people should ask him what this meant, he was to answer them,—"Thus saith the Lord God, Behold I will take the children of Israel from among the heathen whither they be gone, and will gather them on every side, and bring them into their own land: and I will make them ONE NATION in the land upon the mountains of Israel; and ONE KING shall be king to them all; and they shall be *no more two nations, neither shall they be divided into two kingdoms any more at all.*"

Thus, then, shall ALL THE TRIBES OF ISRAEL be gathered from among the countries, and brought safely to the land of their inheritance. And, as ISAIAH prophesied,—the "ROOT OF JESSE . . . . shall stand for an ensign of the people, ... and . . . . the Lord shall set His hand again the second time to recover the remnant of His people which shall be left, from Assyria, and from Egypt, and from Pathros, and from Cush, and from Elam, and from Shinah, and from Hamath, and from the Islands of the Sea. And he shall set up an

ensign for the nations, and shall assemble the outcasts
of ISRAEL, and gather together the dispersed of JUDAH
from the four corners of the earth. The envy also of
Ephraim shall depart, and the adversaries of Judah
shall be cut off: Ephraim shall not envy Judah, and
Judah shall not vex Ephraim."[1]   The "ROOT OF
JESSE" shall stand up to gather Israel His people,—
not like the wicked Antichrist had *partly* gathered them
in unbelief,—but in the full assurance of a holy faith.

Let me enlarge a little upon this. Antichrist will
be, as we have seen, *professedly* the friend of Israel,
and under his protection *many* will be brought again
to the possession of their forefathers. But he will
not bring *all Israel* back. It appears that he will only
have to do with the tribes of JUDAH and BENJAMIN, and
part of LEVI. ZECHARIAH, in the twelfth chapter, says,
—"Jerusalem shall be inhabited again in her own place,
even in Jerusalem. The Lord also shall save *the tents
of Judah first,* that the glory of the house of David, and
the glory of the inhabitants of Jerusalem, do not magnify
themselves against Judah. . . . . And I will pour upon
the house of David and upon the inhabitants of
Jerusalem the spirit of grace and of supplications; and
they shall look upon Me whom they have pierced, and
they shall mourn for Him as one mourneth for his only

---

[1] Isa. xi. 10–13.

son, and shall be in bitterness for Him as one that
is in bitterness for his first-born. In that day shall
there be a great mourning in Jerusalem, as the
mourning of Hadadrimmon in the valley of Megiddon.
And the land shall mourn, every family apart: the
family of the house of David apart, and their wives
apart (here, the representatives of the tribe of JUDAH;)
the family of NATHAN apart, and their wives apart
(here, the representatives of the PROPHETS); the
family of the house of LEVI apart, and their wives
apart (here, the representatives of the tribe of LEVI and
the PRIESTHOOD which pertained thereto); the family
of SHIMEI apart, and their wives apart (here, the
representatives of the tribe of BENJAMIN[1]); ALL THE
FAMILIES THAT REMAIN, every family apart, and their
wives apart" (here, the representatives, probably, of
certain families of other tribes which shall have
returned and taken up their residence in Palestine,
but shall not be found there in such numbers as to be
worthy of especial note). Now we know that the tribes
of Israel, which at the present time inhabit those parts
of the world with which Europeans and the western
Asiatics have more especially to do, are necessarily (with
a small exception, which is not easily discernible) Judah,
Benjamin, and Levi;—*the three tribes* which were taken

---

[1] 2 Sam. xix. 16.

M

captive by Nebuchadnezzar, restored under Zerubbabel, and dispersed under Titus. It is easy to understand the probability that *these* will be restored under THE LAST HEAD OF THE ROMAN EMPIRE, and that when at last the KING shall come "whose right it is to reign," He will take up the cause of Israel's tribes in all the earth, and will "set up an ensign for the nations," and "a sign among them; . . . and they shall bring all" the "brethren of the house of Judah . . . for an offering unto the Lord out of all nations, upon horses, and in chariots, and in litters, and upon mules, and upon swift beasts to" God's "Holy Mountain Jerusalem."[1] And, moreover, that the Lord will "have mercy on" the people of His scattered tribes, and fulfil to them His word, which said, "I will make all my mountains a way, and my highway shall be exalted. Behold these shall come from far; and lo! these from the land of Sinim (China).[2] . . . . The children which thou shalt have

---

[1] Isa. lxvi. 19, 20.

[2] That the country which Isaiah called "Sinim" is the same as that known to us as "China" is, at least, extremely probable. The context plainly shows that it must be a country lying either east or south of Israel. The word is very nearly allied to Sin, or Tcin, or Tshini, by which name the people of China were known to the Arabians and Syrians. Gesenius says, "I understand it to be the land of the Seres, or Chinese, Sinenses." Calmet refers to Mr. Taylor, Drs. Morrison and Hagar, in proof that China is intended. Dr. Kitto says, "Many Biblical geographers think this may possibly denote the Sinese or Chinese, whose country is Sina, China. This view is not void of probability."

after thou hast lost the other shall say again in thine ear, The place is too strait; give place to me, that I may dwell. Then shalt thou say in thine heart, Who hath begotten me these, seeing that I have lost my children and am desolate, a captive, and removing to and fro? And who hath brought up these? Behold I was left alone; *these, where had they been?* Thus saith the Lord God, Behold, I will lift up mine hand to the Gentiles, and set my standard to the people; and they shall bring thy sons in their arms, and thy daughters shall be carried upon their shoulders; and kings shall be their nursing fathers (thy nourishers), and their queens thy nursing mothers : they shall bow down to thee with their face toward the earth, . . . I will contend with him that contendeth with thee, and I will save thy children."[1]

So, when the Lord shall have descended, He shall bow the heart of ALL THE REMNANT to the interests of Israel: and they shall search them out in every nation under heaven, and bring them to their own land, that they may occupy it as an undisturbed possession, "from the wilderness and Lebanon, from the river, the river Euphrates, even unto the uttermost sea." (A vast territory, as we have seen in a former chapter, comprehending, probably, the whole, or nearly the whole peninsula of Arabia.[2]) And thus—"ALL Israel shall

---

[1] Isa. xlix. 11–25.   [2] See Chapter III.

be saved; as it is written, There shall come out of
Zion the Deliverer, that shall turn away ungodliness
from Jacob. . . . . For the gifts and callings of God
are without repentance."[1]

ISRAEL, thus restored in full, will be the people
specially honoured among all the nations of the earth,
as those in whose midst the presence of the Lord will
be made manifest during the Millennial age. In their
Capital He will show forth His glory. In their restored
JERUSALEM will be THE SANCTUARY in which He will
delight, and unto which, as to the hallowed centre of
the world, all nations shall approach with reverence and
joy. THEIR RESTORATION WILL BE THE FIRST GREAT
ACT OF THE MESSIAH, . when, having overthrown the
powers of evil, He will take His seat upon the Throne
as "KING OVER ALL THE EARTH."[2]

Before we speak particularly as to the glorious
manifestation and Divine government of the Messiah,
we will give a passing consideration to the PHYSICAL,
MORAL, and RELIGIOUS STATE of the earth, and of those
people who are to dwell upon it under the triumphant
reign of the GREAT KING.

It is certainly wrong to suppose that the tremendous
conflagration upon which ST. PETER dwells in his
second epistle will take place at the introduction of the

---

[1] Rom. xi. 26–29.   [2] Zech. xiv. 9.

Reign of Peace.[1] It will occur, indeed, *in* "the day of the Lord," but *not at its commencement.* The Millennial age will precede it. We shall see this clearly as we advance with our subjects. Yet GREAT PHYSICAL CHANGES there undoubtedly will be when the Lord shall establish His dominion.

At His coming, when His feet shall stand upon the Mount of Olives, ZECHARIAH tells us that the mountain "shall cleave in the midst thereof towards the east and towards the west, and there shall be a very great valley: and half of the mountain shall remove toward the north, and half of it toward the south."[2] And then, addressing Israel, he says,—"And ye shall flee to the valley of the mountains, for the valley of the mountains shall reach unto Azal; yea, ye shall flee, like as ye fled from before the earthquake in the days of Uzziah, king of Judah." Indeed there will be *good reason* for a hasty flight; for if (as is no doubt the case) AZAL be another name for ASCALON, and a deep valley be formed, reaching from ASCALON across the country, and dividing the Mount of Olives towards the DEAD SEA, we know what must be the issue. The level of the Dead Sea being *many hundreds of feet* below that of the Mediterranean, the waters of the latter sea will speedily rush in. But, to use the language of Major

---

[1] 2 Pet. iii. 10.   [2] Zech. xiv.

Phillips, in his interesting work, *Interpretations of Prophecy*,—"The living waters of the ocean falling a total of nearly eight times the fall of Niagara, with an average descent of twenty-two feet per mile on sixty miles, and entering the Dead Sea at the Northern Extremity, will speedily cause its waters to rise; and while a mighty whirlpool will be created in the vast basin of the Dead Sea, the rising waters will be quietly permeating the drift sands of four thousand years, which now conceal the southern bed of the river Jordan. Yes, as surely as the waters of the Mediterranean will enter the Dead Sea at an angle, and admirably prepared as the geographical construction of its surrounding mountains is to produce a grand gyration, so surely will that gyration of commingled waters rise from a hollow swirl to a mighty, overpowering swell. And when at length the waters stand upon an heap (as Scripture phrases it), and the sustaining power of gyration ceases to uphold, the mass of water falls and separates, and strikes against the surrounding mountain sides. And now, 'Let the sea roar, and the fulness thereof; let the floods clap their hands before the Lord, for He cometh to judge the earth, and the people with His righteousness; and God will make a way in the wilderness, and rivers in the desert.' The tumultuous waters, finding no other outlet, will rush down the

Jordan's bed, cleansing it as in a moment. The Dead
Sea, rising above its desolated shores, will overflow by the
valley of Edom, completing the straits of Azal into the
long Red Sea, by the Gulf of Akabah. Thus JERUSALEM,
BECOMING THE CENTRAL CITY OF THE EARTH, WILL
STAND UPON THE HIGHWAY FOR ALL NATIONS."

Thus we may readily understand how there will be
a fulfilment of divers prophecies, which are otherwise
enveloped in deep mystery. That, for example, in the
ninety-seventh PSALM, which gives us the outline of
the whole course of events immediately consequent upon
the Advent:—"THE LORD REIGNETH, let the earth
rejoice; let the multitude of isles be glad thereof. Clouds
and darkness are round about Him; righteousness and
judgment are the habitation of His throne. A fire
goeth before Him, and burneth up His enemies round
about. His lightnings enlightened the world: the earth
saw and trembled. THE HILLS MELTED LIKE WAX AT
THE PRESENCE OF THE LORD, AT THE PRESENCE OF THE
LORD OF THE WHOLE EARTH. The heavens declare
His righteousness, and all people have seen His glory."
Or again, in the Prophet MICAH, the first chapter,—
"Behold, the Lord cometh forth out of His place, and
will come down and tread upon the high places of the
earth. AND THE MOUNTAINS SHALL BE MOLTEN UNDER
HIM, AND THE VALLEYS SHALL BE CLEFT, AS WAX

BEFORE THE FIRE, AND AS THE WATERS THAT ARE
POURED DOWN A STEEP PLACE." Or again, in HOSEA,
the second chapter, speaking of "that day" wherein
"saith the Lord . . . . thou shalt call me Ishi (my
husband), and shalt call me no more Baali (my Lord);"
it is added,—"Behold I will allure her, and bring her
into the wilderness, and speak comfortably unto her.
And I will give her vineyards *from thence,* and THE
VALLEY OF ACHOR (a valley in the neighbourhood of
Gilgal and Jericho) FOR A DOOR OF HOPE; and she shall
sing there, as in the days of her youth, and as in the
day when she came up out of the land of Egypt."

Or once again;—in JOEL, the third chapter,—"And
it shall come to pass in that day, that the mountains
shall drop down new wine, and the hills shall flow with
milk, and all the rivers of Judah shall flow with waters,
and *a fountain shall come forth of the house of the Lord,
and shall water* THE VALLEY OF SHITTIM." (Shittim
lies E.N.E. of Jerusalem, by the river Jordan.[1])

And thus, Jerusalem will become a city, fit, by reason
of its situation, to be esteemed the capital of the whole
world. Close at hand will be the Dead Sea,—*but with
its waters healed,* so that, as EZEKIEL tells us, "the
fishers shall stand upon it from Engedi even unto
Eneglaim;"[2] and the lake, converted into a vast pool

---

[1] Numb. xxxiii. 49, 50.   [2] Ezek. xlvii. 10.

of shelter for ships, will be entered on the north by the straits flowing from the Mediterranean, and on the south by those which will unite its waters with the Red Sea. With such a change effected, who could select a spot so favourable as JERUSALEM for the situation of the EARTH'S METROPOLIS?

The first verse of the forty-seventh chapter of EZEKIEL relates a remarkable vision of the days of Messiah's kingdom, and says—"He brought me again unto the door of the house (the new Temple); and behold waters issued out from under the threshold of the house *eastward*: for the forefront of the house stood toward the east, and the waters came down from under, from the right side of the house, at the south side of the altar.[1]

---

[1] The well-known engineer, Pierotti, discovered that the present city of Jerusalem is built on several layers of masonry, each layer pertaining to a different age. He saw reason to believe that the lowest layer, which is composed of very large stones, is of the time of Solomon; the next above it of the days of Zerubbabel; the third of the reign of King Herod; the fourth of the time of Justinian, and so on. He found a series of water conduits leading *from the place where the Temple stood* to the valley of Jehoshaphat. He discovered, moreover, a fountain at the pool of Bethesda, from which, upon its being opened, a considerable stream of water began to flow, and has flowed ever since. No one can tell its source, nor can they discover the place which finally receives its flood.

A letter from Jerusalem, quoted some time since in the *Quarterly Journal of Prophecy*, says, "I had a good opportunity of seeing the Temple enclosure. *Wishing to see the water for myself, I went down.*

Then brought he me out of the way of the gate northward, and led me about the way without unto the utter
gate by the way that looketh eastward; and behold
there ran out water on the right side." (That is to say,
perhaps, the waters issuing "from under the threshold
of the Temple," flowed rather to the south of the east.)
"And when the man that had the line in his hand went
forth eastward, he measured a thousand cubits, and he
brought me through the waters; and the waters were
to the ankles. Again he measured a thousand cubits,
and brought me through the waters; the waters were
to the knees. Again he measured a thousand, and
brought me through; the waters were to the loins.
Afterwards he measured a thousand; and it was a river
that I could not pass over.[1] . . . Then said he unto me,
These waters issue out *towards the east country* (that is,
in the direction of the northern point of the Dead Sea),

By the side of El-Aksa is the entrance to the subterranean water. You
descend a few steps, and then jump into a hole. Before you is a door
cut out of the rock. You pass this doorway, and descend a flight of
broad steps to the edge of the water, which is delightful, very cold, about
four feet deep, and pebbly at the bottom, as if it were spring water.
It is not known how far it extends. It branches off in every direction;
and in the water are large irregular pillars."

[1] This will, no doubt, be a stream of spring water, flowing in a s.e.
direction from the Temple, until it meets the Straits which are to cross
the country from the Mediterranean to the north of the Dead Sea.

and down into the Desert (or Plain), and go into the
Sea (the Dead Sea); which (waters) being brought forth
into the Sea, the waters (of the Sea) *shall be healed.*
And it shall come to pass, that everything that liveth,
which moveth whithersoever the rivers shall come, shall
live; and there shall be a very great multitude of fish,
because these waters shall come thither: for they shall
be healed; and everything shall live whither the river
cometh. And it shall come to pass, that the fishers
shall stand upon it from Engedi even to Eneglaim: they
shall be a place to spread forth nets; their fish shall
be according to their kinds AS THE FISH OF THE GREAT
SEA (the Mediterranean), exceeding many." Surely no
one can consider this to be mere *figurative* language. It
speaks for itself, that *there shall be material physical
changes in the neighbourhood of Jerusalem;* changes which
shall place the city in a position *far* more favourable
than that which it at present occupies.

Nor are these all the changes which are to affect the
neighbourhood of Zion when the Lord shall come. For
we read in the fourteenth chapter of ZECHARIAH that—
"All the land shall be turned as a plain, from GEBA
to RIMMON, south of Jerusalem, and it shall be lifted
up." Now GEBA was a city of Benjamin, a few miles
north of Jerusalem;[1] and RIMMON was a city of Judah

---

[1] Josh. xxviii. 24; xxi. 17.

on the southern boundary.[1] Thus *a vast extent of table
land* will be ,formed, for an important purpose, which
will be brought forward presently. For the moment
let it suffice to mention it, and pass on to observe
changes which will take place elsewhere. We read
that desert places are to teem with vegetable life and
beauty. For example—Idumea is spoken of; and after
its judgments are proclaimed, it is added—"The desert
shall rejoice and blossom as the rose. It shall blossom
abundantly, and rejoice even with joy and singing; the
glory of Lebanon shall be given unto it, the excellency
of Carmel and Sharon, ... the parched ground shall
become a pool, and the thirsty land springs of water,
. . . and an highway shall be there;" and this shall be
when "the ransomed of the Lord shall return and come
to Zion with songs and everlasting joy upon their heads."[2]
And so again the Lord declares (but not, it would appear,
of any one place particularly),—"Behold, I will do a
new thing; now it shall spring forth; shall ye not know
it? I will even make a way in the wilderness, and
rivers in the desert. The beasts of the field shall
honour Me, the dragons and the owls: because I gave
waters in the wilderness and rivers in the desert, to give
drink to My people, My chosen."

True, it *may* be only the land of Israel (as it shall

---

[1] Josh. xv. 21–32.   [2] Isa. xxxiv. and xxxv.

then be) which will become the subject of these changes,[1] but there is reason to believe that they will be *general*, for the *whole world* is evidently called to the rejoicings of the millennial period; and the Lord is not to be King over Israel only, but "OVER ALL THE EARTH." It must be enough for us, however, that we accept the limits of the Scripture word. For the rest, the Lord will show us in His own good time.

While thus speaking of the physical changes which will affect man's comfort, we must not overlook what is said so plainly about a *wondrous transformation* of which those LOWER ANIMALS, which now prey upon each other, and are wont to make attack upon the life of men, will be the subjects. How it *can be* I will not stay to ask; "WITH GOD ALL THINGS ARE POSSIBLE." That it *will be* is distinctly stated; and it is enough. These ravenous beasts *shall never more destroy* when the Redeemer's reign of peace shall be established; for the mouth of the Lord hath spoken it. He who could first *form*, can when He pleases, *re-form;* and RE-FORM HE WILL. "Behold, I create new heavens and a new earth: and the former shall not be remembered, nor come into mind . . . . The wolf

---

[1] The promised land of Israel will comprehend Idumea, and vast tracts of wilderness.

and the lamb shall feed together, and the lion shall eat straw like the bullock; and dust shall be the serpent's meat. They shall not hurt nor destroy in all My holy mountain, saith the Lord."[1]

WHEN SHALL ALL THIS BE? The same prophet, ISAIAH, by whom these last words were spoken, tells us in the eleventh chapter that it shall be *when* the "Rod out of the stem of Jesse," and the "Branch out of his roots," shall come forth; that King who shall "with righteousness .. judge the poor, and reprove with equity for the meek of the earth," the girdle of whose loins, moreover, shall be "righteousness," and "faithfulness the girdle of His reins:"—*when* "the Lord shall set His hand *again the second time* to recover the remnant of His people which shall be left, . . . the outcasts of Israel and the dispersed of Judah:"—*when* "the envy also of Ephraim shall depart, and the adversaries of Judah shall be cut off," and "Ephraim shall not envy Judah," and "Judah shall not vex Ephraim:"—and *when* the word shall sound forth from the length and breadth of earth, "Cry out and shout, thou inhabitant of Zion; for great is the Holy One of Israel in the midst of thee,"—THEN shall be THAT HAPPY DAY OF PEACE, among the wonders of which it is declared in agreement with

[1] Isa. lxv. 17-25.

the quotation just made,—" The wolf also shall dwell
with the lamb, and the leopard shall lie down with
the kid; and the calf, and the young lion, and the
fatling together; and a little child shall lead them.
And the cow and the bear shall feed; their young
ones shall lie down together; and the lion shall eat
straw like the ox.   And the sucking child shall play on
the hole of the asp, and the weaned child shall put
his hand on the cockatrice's den.   They shall not hurt
nor destroy in all My holy mountain; for the earth shall
be full of the knowledge of the Lord, as the waters cover
the sea."[1]   Surely it cannot be the part of WISDOM to
cavil at, or *explain away*, or try to *spiritualize* such
passages as these.   It is better to *receive with meekness*
what the Lord has spoken, and *submissively adore*.   *Our*
IMPOSSIBILITIES are *God's* SIMPLICITIES.   How foolish
many a *learned reasoner* of earth will look in the
presence of his *untutored neighbour* in the day of Christ!
The *garb of his philosophy*—his *wise conclusions*—his
" *cannot be*" and "*must be*" all departed; and his soul,
through earthly wisdom, standing *wrapped in folly;*
while that man of simple, childlike faith, which had
been wont on earth to lay his hand upon his mouth,
and meekly listen to the Word of God; *and not having
seen or even understood*, yet had believed, and prayed for

[1] Isa. x'. and lxv.

light, and rendered thanks to God for every little gleam from heaven,—*shall stand forth adorned in wisdom, such as the All-Wise will look upon with approbation!*

Let us now consider MAN'S ESTATE during the Lord's Reign of Peace.

We must not confound the *Millennial* State of which we are now speaking with the state of *Final Glory*. In the Millennial period the earth will be inhabited just as it has been throughout previous ages; children will be born, and those who shall have fulfilled their years will die. There will be *peace*, but not *perfection;* comparative, but *not perfect* righteousness. The change will be great, but not a change like that from Earth to *Heaven*. It will be *Earth still*, and Man *in fallen nature* will be earth's inhabitant. Yet Man will undergo a change; his state will not be just what it is now. But we will see what God has taught concerning this. Let us refer to the sixty-fifth chapter of ISAIAH, in which that day is spoken of, wherein "the wolf and the lamb shall feed together, . . . and they shall not hurt nor destroy." Here we find also the grand promise which God made to Israel:—"I will rejoice in Jerusalem, and joy in My people: and the voice of weeping shall be no more heard in her, nor the voice of crying. There shall be no more thence an infant of days, nor an old man that hath not filled his days; *for the child shall die an hundred years old.* . . . . And they shall build houses and inhabit them, and they shall plant vineyards and eat the fruit of them. They shall not build, and *another* inhabit; they shall not plant, and *another* eat: for *as the days of a tree* are the days of my people; and *mine elect shall long enjoy the work of their own hands."*

So it is evident that there will be DEATH ("The child shall *die*"). But it is evident also that the life of man will be *prolonged*, perhaps as in the days of the early Patriarchs (" as the days of a tree are the days of my people"), so that the constitution of man will have received a new supply of strength. As he passes on through life, however, there will be warning voices telling him that this is not his home. He will not wholly escape sickness: wherefore *trees* are spoken of as abounding by the waters of the regenerated Israel, of which the fruit "shall be for meat, and the leaf thereof for MEDICINE."[1]

But observe what is said about THINGS SPIRITUAL in this Reign of Peace.

We have just seen that man will be the subject of affliction, sickness, and death, during the Millennial period. This would *not* be if he were *sinless;* for *death* is emphatically declared to be WAGES OF SIN.[2] Indeed,

---

[1] Ezek. xlvii. 12.   [2] Rom. vi. 23.

N

the Prophet Isaiah, in the chapter from which we
have just now been quoting, very plainly intimates
that there shall be sin, saying,—The sinner, being a
hundred years old, shall be accursed."

Zechariah, too, leads us to the same conclusion in
the latter part of the fourteenth chapter, where he says
—"And it shall come to pass that every one that is
left of all the nations which came against Jerusalem
shall even go up from year to year to worship the King,
the Lord of Hosts, and to keep the Feast of Tabernacles.
And it shall be that *whoso will not come up of all the
families of the earth unto Jerusalem to worship the King,
the Lord of Hosts, even upon them shall be no rain.* And
if the family of Egypt go not up, and come not, that
have no rain, there shall be the plague wherewith the
Lord will smite the heathen that come not up to keep
the Feast of Tabernacles. *This shall be the punishment
of Egypt, and the punishment of all nations that come
not up to keep the Feast of Tabernacles.*" So, doubtless,
there will be *sin,* and *curse* because of sin. Yet sin
will not be rampant. Open transgression will be *rare ;*
for, although mankind will still retain the flesh, as of
old,—unregenerated, unaltered, as prone as ever to
iniquity,—so that therein will dwell "no good thing,"
and the unholy law thereof will be as truly adverse to
"the law" of the regenerated mind as it is now, or as

it was when the Apostle wrote concerning it:[1] yet the *prompting power* will be removed; Satan will be bound; and all temptation from the spiritual powers of evil will have ceased. Moreover, there will be *no room* for unbelief or doubt; "for the knowledge of the glory of the Lord shall cover the earth, as the waters cover the seas."[2] And besides this the righteous government of the Almighty King will favour righteous dealing among all people. The evidence of perfect love controlling all things with regard to man, will favour kindly feeling, charitable action, and an open, generous demeanour.

Thus, although the earth, beneath the sway of the long-promised sceptre, *will not be transformed into heaven*, yet it will be greatly changed, and become, as it were, "a *new* earth," in which righteousness, peace, confidence, and love will everywhere abound; and wherein those who will not give their hearts to God will be but few and hidden.

Let us look higher, and consider for a while THE KING OF KINGS and His associates in government. "Behold a King shall reign in righteousness, and Princes shall execute judgment."[3] "Behold the days come, saith the Lord, that I will raise unto David a

---

[1] Rom. vii. 14-25.   [2] Isa. xi. 9; Hab. ii. 14.
[3] Isa. xxxii. 1.

Righteous Branch, and a King shall reign and prosper, and shall execute judgment and justice in the earth. In His days Judah shall be saved, and Israel shall dwell safely : and this is His name whereby He shall be called, THE LORD OUR RIGHTEOUSNESS."[1] He "shall reign in Mount Zion and in Jerusalem and among His ancients gloriously,"[2] and He "shall be King over all the earth;"[3] for He shall receive the heathen for His inheritance, and the uttermost parts of the earth for His possession ; and, having broken the wicked as with a rod of iron, dashed them in pieces like a potter's vessel,[4] and destroyed them with the sword of His justice, He shall enter upon full and glorious possession of the world, and be acknowledged by all nations to be "KING OF KINGS and LORD OF LORDS." "His name shall be called WONDERFUL, COUNSELLOR, THE MIGHTY GOD, THE EVERLASTING FATHER, THE PRINCE OF PEACE."[5]

In speaking of His reign, we must confess a difficulty.

We have seen, I believe, clearly, that the Lord will descend from heaven *in His Manhood;* and that *as Son of Man* He will "stand upon the Mount of Olives," and "sit upon the throne of His glory." Indeed, it must be clear to every candid reader of the prophecies, that

---

[1] Jer. xxiii. 5. 6.   [2] Isa. xxiv. 23.
[3] Zech. xiv. 9.   [4] Ps. ii.   [5] Isa. ix. 6.

the Lord will, *in His human nature*, rendered wonderfully glorious in the glory of the Father, stand upon the earth; and that as the King, *whose right it is*, He will ascend the throne of David, both to order and establish the kingdom of that honoured prince, with judgment and with justice. The testimony is of the fullest and the plainest kind, and cannot be gainsayed.

But are we *obliged*, therefore, to understand that the Lord Jesus Christ will really make the earth again His *dwelling-place*?—that He will actually, and for the period of a thousand years, *take this world for His abode?* He *may* indeed; but I do not think the evidence is strong enough for us to say "HE WILL." It appears to my mind very certain that HE WILL NOT make earth the *residence* of His glorified body; but that He will, for the period of the Millennial age, inhabit *the Jerusalem above*,—the "NEW JERUSALEM," which is to come out of heaven from God,[1] of which the glory of God and of the Lamb is the light. Of this "New Jerusalem" we shall have to speak particularly in another chapter. Let it suffice for the present that it will very probably be *within sight of the inhabitants of earth*, and will be known as the glorious abode of Christ and the entire vast company of His risen saints; so that there will be

[1] Rev. xxi.

a constant evidence afforded of the *reality* of the Redeemer's reign, and of the *bliss of His redeemed and saved
people*. The residence of the Great King in this abode
of glory need not prevent His acting toward mankind
as 'He was wont to act in days of early innocence, when
He came down and visited the Garden of Eden, that
He might converse with our first parents as their FRIEND
and COUNSELLOR. Surely no one will object to the
idea that He may condescend to such an intercourse
again, descending from above, from time to time, to
visit the Millennial earth, that men may be inspired with
higher confidence and purer love. The tone of the
prophetic word most certainly shows favour to the
opinion that He will do so. But, if so, then we need
not pause to question *how* or *where* a *fitting Residence*
shall be prepared by God for His abode and that of
all the multitude of His redeemed people upon the
hallowed height (a matter, of course, full of serious
difficulties); but we can hold the doctrine of His
reign as King over the whole earth, and in a special
manner, as the KING OF ISRAEL, and of our reign
with Him.

We have material aid in support of this view from
the two Prophets, JEREMIAH and EZEKIEL, which we
shall do well to observe.

To prepare ourselves for their remarkable assertions,

we will call to mind the testimony afforded to us in Scripture to the fact that the GLORIFIED SAINTS *shall occupy important places in the government of Israel and of the world.* OUR SAVIOUR told His apostles that it should be so. "In the regeneration," said He, "when the SON OF MAN shall sit on the throne of His glory, *ye also shall sit on twelve thrones, judging the twelve tribes of Israel.*"[1] The Apostle PAUL, rebuking the Corinthians for divisions which they suffered to exist, demanded of them,—"Do ye not know that *the Saints shall judge the world?*"[2] And JOHN, in the twentieth chapter of the REVELATION, tells us,—"I saw *thrones, and they sat upon them, and judgment was given unto them;* and I saw the souls of them that were beheaded for the witness of Jesus, and for the Word of God, and which had not worshipped the beast, neither his image; neither had received his mark upon their foreheads, or in their hands; *and they lived and reigned with Christ a thousand years.*" It is quite certain, then, that judgment shall, in some sense and degree, "*be delivered unto the Saints,*" and that, as DANIEL tells us,—"The kingdom and dominion, and the greatness of the kingdom under the whole heaven, shall be given *to the people of the Saints of the Most High,* whose kingdom is an everlasting kingdom, and all dominions shall serve and obey Him."[3]

[1] Matt. xix. 28. [2] 1 Cor. vi. 2. [3] Dan. vii. 27.

In speaking of the share which shall be granted to the saints of Jesus in the Millennial kingdom, we must not omit to notice a point of very interesting, and—to Israel especially—of heart-stirring kind. I mean THE VICE-ROYALTY OF THE RISEN DAVID. This is the subject to which I referred as advanced by JEREMIAH and EZEKIEL in aid of the doctrine that the Lord shall indeed reign over the earth, but having His abode in the "New Jerusalem" above, and of His saints reigning with Him.

In JEREMIAH, the thirtieth chapter, we find the Prophet descanting in language which we have already quoted, upon Jacob's trouble and deliverance. In the eighth verse we read thus—"It shall come to pass in that day, saith the Lord of Hosts, that I will break *his* yoke[1] from off thy neck, and will burst thy bonds, and strangers shall no more serve themselves of him: but they shall serve THE LORD THEIR GOD, and *David, their king, whom I will raise up unto them.* Therefore, fear thou not, O My servant Jacob, saith the Lord."

Now if this passage stood alone, we should be tempted, perhaps, to pass it over without any great regard; for its subject is *extraordinary*, and the idea would be

---

[1] The yoke of *some one* who shall have dominion in "the day of Jacob's trouble." The context shows that he is "the Antichrist." Read Jeremiah, chapters xxx. and xxxi.

readily encouraged that some *hidden* interpretation must be correct, instead of that which is at once apparent. We should be tempted to consider, perhaps, that the name "DAVID" was given to CHRIST, He being David's "Root and Offspring." But the passage we have quoted is supported far too strongly to allow of this. It is evidently to be taken as it stands. In the thirty-fourth chapter of EZEKIEL we find much said about the Restoration of the Tribes of Israel, when the Lord "will gather them from the countries, and will bring them to their own land, and feed them upon the mountains of Israel." Many, and replete with consolation, are the words which are spoken about those who shall be brought from the dispersion. The Lord calls them His sheep, and Himself their careful owner, saying,— "I will save My flock, and they shall be no more a prey; and I will judge between cattle and cattle. And I will set up *one Shepherd* over them, and he shall feed them, even *My servant* DAVID: he shall feed them, and he shall be their shepherd. And I THE LORD *will be* THEIR GOD, *and* MY SERVANT DAVID *a Prince among them*. I the Lord have spoken it." Now, certainly, in this place it is *not possible* for "DAVID" to be put for "THE LORD," because the Lord speaks of Himself *separately*. "I THE LORD will be THEIR GOD, and MY SERVANT DAVID a Prince among them."

"In the thirty-seventh chapter, where the subject of Israel's restoration is again introduced, God declares, —"I will make them (Israel and Judah) ONE NATION, in the land, upon the mountains of Israel; and ONE KING shall be KING TO THEM ALL: and they shall be no more two nations, neither shall they be divided into two kingdoms any more at all: neither shall they defile themselves any more with idols, nor with their detestable things, nor with any of their transgressions; . . so they shall be My people, and I will be THEIR GOD,"—He adds—"AND DAVID MY SERVANT shall be KING over them, and they shall all have one shepherd: they shall also walk in My judgments, and observe My statutes and do them. And they shall dwell in the land that I have given unto Jacob My servant, wherein your fathers have dwelt: and they shall dwell therein, even they and their children, and their children's children for ever; and MY SERVANT DAVID SHALL BE THEIR PRINCE FOR EVER . . . My tabernacle also shall be with them; yea, I will be THEIR GOD, and they shall be My people."

I do not think that any language can speak plainer than this. *Why should we assume that it is figurative?* Would we presume to say *"It cannot be"* when God has thus repeatedly and unequivocally declared "IT SHALL BE"? Nay, rather, let us here, as elsewhere, take God's word to be the simple truth, whether it agree or disagree with our ideas. Indeed, what *friend of Israel* would *desire* to explain such a declaration otherwise than as it stands? For what should be a greater joy to the Twelve Tribes, when in possession of their Covenant-inheritance, than to find their ancient, well-beloved DAVID also given them TO BE THEIR KING? Who is he who would not praise the Lord for such amazing proof of love towards Israel?

We may conclude, then, that KING DAVID AND THE OTHER SAINTS OF CHRIST shall occupy appointed places in the government and judgment of this world. Like Christ it is quite possible they may not *live on earth;* they may, perhaps, only *visit* it from time to time. No information has been given as to this; nor is it needful we should know particulars concerning it, until the day of Christ arrives. Let this suffice,—THE LORD SHALL REIGN SUPREME, the KING OF KINGS. DAVID, as the chief Viceroy of Christ, shall be the KING OF ISRAEL. The other SAINTS shall also REIGN WITH CHRIST, and JUDGE THE WORLD. So then, as the Prophet bids, let us "Behold, a King shall reign in righteousness, and Princes shall rule in judgment. And a man shall be as an hiding-place from the wind, and a covert from the tempest; as rivers of water in a dry place; as the shadow of a great rock in a weary land. And the eyes of them that see shall not be dim : and the ears of them that hear shall hearken. The heart also of the rash shall understand knowledge, and the tongue of the stammerers shall be ready to speakly plainly."[1]

We must speak of another matter; viz., the RE-LIGIOUS WORSHIP during the Reign of Peace.

I do not see how it is possible to read the word of Prophecy concerning the Millennial age, without arriving at the conclusion that A TEMPLE WILL BE ERECTED AT JERUSALEM, in which, during that happy period, the Lord shall manifest His glory, and declare His presence with His people.

Concerning this Temple, its glory and its service, much is told us in the Scriptures, which we must proceed carefully to observe.

We have already spoken of the Temple which Israel will erect after their partial restoration under Antichrist. *That temple will undoubtedly be destroyed* at the coming of the Lord ;—for not only will a great earthquake then divide the Mount of Olives, and form a chasm from Ascalon to the valley of Achor, but also (as we have seen in the earlier part of this chapter) "all the land shall be turned *as a plain,* from GEBA to RIMMON, south of Jerusalem, and it shall be *lifted up ;*"[2] so that utter destruction will probably befall every edifice in or near the City.

---

[1] Isa. xxxii. 1-4.   [2] Zech. xiv. 4-10.

But, independently of this, it is quite evident that the Temple which the Jews will erect, or set about erecting, on their first restoration, will not be the Temple which is to adorn Jerusalem of the Millennial age. At least, it is exceedingly improbable that it will be so, by reason of the *vast dimensions* given for the Millennial Temple and City, and the *brief period* (consisting of seven years only)[1] which is to be allotted to the Jews, from their return under Antichrist to the dawn of the Great Day of God. Indeed, how much more reasonable is the supposition, that when the Lord shall come and establish His dominion over the whole earth, if a Temple be required in the renewed Jerusalem, it should be erected *then !*

No doubt, we are to understand that when the Lord has come, and has established His kingdom, and manifested forth His glory in the sight of all men, HE WILL DIRECT THE BUILDING OF A TEMPLE AS THE GRAND CENTRE OF HIS WORSHIP, AND THE PLACE WHERE HE MAY CHIEFLY HOLD COMMUNION WITH THE SONS OF MEN. The wondrously exalted plain from Geba to Rimmon will form a site "beautiful for situation," upon which a city of great magnitude will be erected, the chief attraction in which will be this Temple of the Lord, in which will be displayed the glorious Shekinah of His

[1] Chapter III., page 101.

presence. And thus Jerusalem, "the city of the great King," will be the "JOY OF THE WHOLE EARTH." Concerning this we must speak at some length.

The Lord had shown His servant EZEKIEL the whole outline of events connected with the restoration of Israel, the reunion of the Twelve Tribes, the reign of the risen David, and other matters in which God's people, in the "last great day," will have intimate concern. And now, as the remarkable prophecy draws towards its close, the Lord would give His servant the most minute instructions with regard both to the City and the Temple to which we have referred.

In the fortieth chapter, the prophet is brought before us standing in the land of Israel "upon a very high mountain, by which was, *as the frame of a city*, towards the south." A man was by the prophet "with a line of flax in his hand and a measuring reed;" and he commenced a measurement of *the Temple*, which was in the city. The length of the reed with which he measured was six cubits and six hand-breadths. Therefore, about ten feet six inches (taking the cubit at eighteen inches and the hand-breadth at three inches). The man began by the measurement of a wall which was round about the house, on which were erected many small chambers; and pursuing his work, measuring the courts, the gateways, the porches, and at length the main building of the Temple itself. Now the extreme length of each side of the surrounding wall was five hundred reeds, or about five thousand two hundred and fifty feet, that is to say, *a mile* all but thirty·feet. This would make the Temple and its enclosure about equal to the greatest extent reached by the entire ancient city of Jerusalem, the circumference of which (according to Josephus) was thirty-three stadia, or three and a half geographical miles, nearly.[1]

I must refer my readers to their Bibles for the whole details of the wondrous Temple. The prophet has minutely given them, and his language is so plain that no interpreter is needed.

To one point, however, I would direct attention, since it has been a matter of interesting inquiry to many students of the prophecies. Will there be, or will there not be, A RESTITUTION OF THE MOSAIC SACRIFICES in the Millennial Temple? Sacrifices *commemorative* of what Christ HAS DONE, instead of (as they were of old) *the types* of what Christ WAS TO DO?

Concerning this, as every other subject, the plain

---

[1] The measurement of the Millennial *Jerusalem* is given in the 48th chapter of Ezekiel. The length of each of the four sides is four thousand five hundred measures (*i.e.* measuring reeds of 10½ feet): equal therefore to forty-seven thousand two hundred and fifty feet, or nearly NINE MILES. So that the whole circumference of the city is to be about THIRTY-SIX MILES.

assertions of the Word of God must be CONCLUSIVE. We are not to refuse our credence to the things revealed because *we cannot see* how they will harmonize with other matters in the Lord's economy. The spirit which the zealous Peter manifested when he said, "Be it far from Thee, Lord, this shall not be unto Thee," was not good. The Lord rebuked it, saying, "Get thee behind Me, Satan, thou art an offence unto Me; for thou savourest not the things that be of God, but those that be of men."[1]

Being resolved, then, to take the Word of God *as we find it*, we will follow the course of those chapters—the *fortieth* to the *forty-sixth* of Ezekiel, inclusive—which describe the Temple; noting those passages which have immediate reference to this matter. Taking first, then, the *fortieth* chapter, we pass over the minute particulars as to chambers, gates, windows, and ornaments, until we reach the *thirty-eighth verse*, from which place and onward we read as follows:—"And the chambers, and the entries thereof, were by the posts of the gates, *where they washed the burnt-offering*. And in the porch of the gate were two tables on this side, and two tables on that side, *to slay thereon the burnt-offering, and the sin-offering, and the trespass-offering.* . . . . Four tables were on this side, and four tables on that

[1] Matt. xvi. 22, 23.

side, by the side of the gate; eight tables, *whereupon they slew their sacrifices;* and the four tables were of hewn stone for the *burnt-offering*, of a cubit and a half long, and a cubit and a half broad, and one cubit high: *whereupon also they laid the instruments wherewith they slew the burnt-offering and the sacrifice.* And within were hooks an hand broad, fastened round about; and *upon the tables was the flesh of the offering."* But again let us pass on, until we come to the *thirteenth verse* of the *forty-second chapter*, where it is declared of certain chambers, that therein "the priests that approach unto the LORD shall eat the most holy things; there they shall lay the most holy things, and *the meat offering, and the sin-offering, and the trespass-offering."* Then passing on to the *next chapter*, at the *thirteenth verse*, we find minute instructions given about the altar and the sacrifices, which are more conclusive still. "And these are the measures of the altar after the cubits (the cubit is a cubit of an hand breadth), ... the altar shall be four cubits; and from the altar and upward shall be four horns. And the altar shall be twelve cubits long, twelve broad, and square in the four squares thereof. .... And he said unto me, Son of man, thus saith the Lord God. These are the ordinances of the altar, in the day when they shall make it, *to offer burnt-offerings thereon and to*

o

sprinkle blood thereon. And thou shalt give to the Priests, the Levites that be of the seed of Zadok, which approach unto Me, to minister unto Me, saith the Lord God, *a young bullock for a sin-offering.* And *thou shalt take of the blood thereof,* and put it on the four horns of it, and on the four corners of the settle, and upon the border round about; thus shalt thou cleanse and purge it. Thou shalt take *the bullock also of the sin-offering,* and he shall burn it in the appointed place of the house, without the sanctuary. And on the second day *thou shalt offer a kid of the goats without blemish for a sin-offering;* and they shall cleanse the altar, as they did cleanse it with the bullock. And when thou hast made an end of cleansing it, *thou shalt offer a young bullock without blemish, and a ram out of the flock without blemish.* And thou shalt offer them before the Lord. . . . . Seven days shalt thou prepare every day a goat for a sin-offering: they shall also prepare a young bullock, and .a ram out of the flock, without blemish . . . . and when these days are expired, it shall be that upon the eighth day, and so forward, *the priests shall make your burnt-offerings upon the altar, and your peace-offerings;* AND I WILL ACCEPT YOU, SAITH THE LORD GOD." But further, let us note the language of the *forty-fifth chapter.* Here again we have the particular sacrifices which are to be offered brought before us, and " THE

PRINCE "[1] is spoken of as having an important office to fulfil in connexion with the offerings. If we refer to the *fifteenth verse*, we read thus—" One lamb out of the flock, one out of two hundred, out of the fat pastures of Israel, for a meat-offering, and for a burnt-offering, and for peace-offerings, to make reconciliation for them, saith the Lord God. All the people of the land shall give this oblation *for the Prince* in Israel. And it shall be *the Prince's part to give burnt-offerings, and meat-offerings, and drink-offerings,* in the feasts, and in the new moons, and in the Sabbaths, in all solemnities of the house of Israel : *He shall prepare* the sin-offering, and the meat-offering, and the burnt-offering, and the peace-offering, to make reconciliation for the house of Israel." But we need not quote further, though there remains much wherewith to strengthen our position, and give force to our assertion, THAT GOD HAS TOLD US PLAINLY, THAT THERE SHALL BE SACRIFICES ACTUALLY OFFERED UPON THE ALTAR OF THE LORD IN THAT TEMPLE WHICH IS TO BE THE GLORY OF THE MILLENNIAL JERUSALEM—SACRIFICES COMMEMORATIVE OF THE SEVERAL POINTS AND BEARINGS OF THE FINISHED WORK OF THE LORD JESUS

---

[1] Probably "the Prince" is David, as we have seen in commenting on the thirty-seventh chapter, where we read—"My servant David shall be *their prince* for ever."

CHRIST. If EZEKIEL's language in this case be *figurative*, I know not where in the whole Word of God we can find any as to which we have a right to say that *it is literal*.

But we must refer to the books of *other* Prophets before we close the subject of this Temple and its services, and see if they give any information which will throw light upon it.

ISAIAH speaks plainly of the Millennial TEMPLE in the *second chapter*, as an exalted place into which "all nations shall flow," and from which the law and the word of the Lord shall go forth. In the *sixty-sixth* chapter also we find God speaking of the *Priests* and *Levites* whom He will appoint in the day of Israel's restoration, when the tribes shall be brought out of all nations as "an offering unto the Lord."

JEREMIAH tells us in the thirteenth chapter,—"Thus saith the Lord, Behold, I will bring again the captivity of Jacob's tents, and have mercy on his dwelling-places; *and the city shall be builded* upon her own heap, and *the palace* shall remain after the fashion thereof. And out of them shall proceed thanksgiving. . . . . In the latter days ye shall consider it." Again in the *thirty-third* chapter,—"*Neither shall the Priests, the Levites, want a man before me to offer burnt-offerings, and to kindle meat-offerings, and to do sacrifice continually.*"

MICAH speaks of it in the *fourth chapter* of his prophecy almost in the same words as those which were used by Isaiah,—"In the last day it shall come to pass that the mountain of *the House of the Lord* shall be established in the top of the mountains . . . and many nations shall come and say, Come, and let us go up to the mountain of the Lord, and *to the House of the God of Jacob*, and He will teach us of His ways."

In HAGGAI, the *second chapter*, God declares,—"Yet once, it is a little while, and I will shake the heavens, and the earth, and the sea, and the dry land; and I will shake all nations, and the Desire of all nations shall come; and I will fill this House with glory, saith the Lord of Hosts. . . . . *The glory of this latter House shall be greater than the former*, saith the Lord of Hosts; and in this place I will give peace, saith the Lord of Hosts." Surely this was only, as it were, *typically* fulfilled by the *first* coming of the Lord. A more perfect accomplishment is demanded by the prophet's language.

ZECHARIAH also speaks very plainly, in the *last chapter* of his prophecy, where he declares the judgment against all the families of the earth, which "go not up from year to year to worship the King, the Lord of Hosts, at Jerusalem, and to keep the Feast of

Tabernacles," and where also he says, "In that day shall there be upon the bells of the horses Holiness unto the Lord; and the pots *in the Lord's House* shall be like the bowls before the altar. Yea, every pot in Jerusalem and in Judah shall be Holiness unto the Lord of Hosts; and *all they that sacrifice* shall come and take of them, and seethe therein: and in that day there shall be no more the Canaanite *in the House of the Lord of Hosts.*"

Such is the testimony which it has pleased God to afford respecting the Millennial Temple and the Services thereof. We find that EZEKIEL does not stand, by any means, without support. To him, indeed, was committed the *accurate description;* but other prophets were to add corroborative testimony, more or less powerful. And now may we not ask with confidence, "WHO ART THOU THAT REPLIEST AGAINST GOD?" Nay, *let not poor erring man* REPLY, but wait, depending with a simple confidence upon what the Lord has said, till he behold more clearly than EZEKIEL in the vision, the vast glory of the King of kings, and rejoice with all His people in the complete display of those transcendent wonders of His love and power, which will be certainly revealed before the eyes of all whose hearts shall be prepared to render hallowed praise, and join the angels in their blissful adoration.

In such an aspect, O how great and glorious does the *day of Israel's rest* appear! How wonderfully honoured and how richly blest! Their King reigning in unspotted righteousness; their Princes executing perfect judgment; their Priests and Levites carrying out the will of God in truth;—the presence of their Lord—the Lord of Hosts—among them; His glory filling all His House; and His word declaring it to be —"THE PLACE OF MY THRONE, AND THE PLACE OF THE SOLES OF MY FEET, WHERE I WILL DWELL IN THE MIDST OF THE CHILDREN OF ISRAEL FOR EVER," and adding, "AND MY HOLY NAME SHALL THE HOUSE OF ISRAEL NO MORE DEFILE."[1]

But, further, we must observe how happy too will be the condition of ALL GENTILE NATIONS. Their swords beaten into ploughshares, and their spears into pruning-hooks. No warfare learned. Peace everywhere. The knowledge of God's glory in every family. No man finding need to say to any of his fellows, "Know the Lord;" because all shall know Him, from the least to the greatest.

So, for the predicted period of ONE THOUSAND YEARS, shall the Redeemer's kingdom on the earth endure in undisturbed righteousness and peace. Yet this shall

---

[1] Ezek. xliii. 7.

be but, as it were, the entrance-gate of a more glorious period of His reign;—for "OF THE INCREASE OF HIS GOVERNMENT AND PEACE THERE SHALL BE NO END, UPON THE THRONE OF DAVID, AND UPON HIS KINGDOM, TO ORDER IT AND TO ESTABLISH IT, WITH JUDGMENT, AND WITH JUSTICE, FROM HENCEFORTH EVEN FOR EVER."

CHAPTER VII.

The Final Outbreak of Evil.

"Thus saith the Lord God, It shall also come to pass that at the same time shall things come into thy mind, and thou shalt think an evil thought: and thou shalt say, I will go up to the land of unwalled villages; I will go to them that are at rest, that dwell safely, all of them dwelling without walls, and having neither bars nor gates, to take a spoil, and to take a prey."—EZEK. xxxviii. 10–12.

THE LORD'S GREAT DAY, so rich in righteousness and peace, will (as we have seen) endure in its MERIDIAN SPLENDOUR for "A THOUSAND YEARS." During this long period the world is to enjoy rest indeed. The Day which dawned in fearful judgment, shall find good reason to rejoice because of universal piety and undisturbed repose beneath Immanuel's sceptre. But the EVENING of this great and glorious Day must follow; for this world is not designed to be our everlasting home. Therefore the deep shadows which foretell approaching night, will be extended over all things earthly.

THE EVENING OF THE LORD'S GREAT DAY will open
subjects which are to occupy both this and the succeed-
ing chapter.

In dwelling on the peculiar features of the Saviour's
Reign of Peace, we were, I hope, careful to observe
that, although the Word of God has said so much
concerning the extent to which true righteousness will
prevail, yet it has revealed with perfect clearness, that
*the sinful nature of the fallen Adam will remain, so that
there will be a tendency to do evil as great as that which
exists now.* But inasmuch as Satan will be bound, and
suffered to deceive mankind no longer, this tendency
will be deprived of its most powerful instigator; and
since faith will be in measure lost in sight, and in-
centives to perform the will of God will, in a peculiar
manner, be presented to the eye of man, *the fleshly power
of evil will be in great measure latent.* None perhaps
will be able to charge the converted people of the Lord
with inconsistency; and those who may remain yet
unregenerate, will walk *orderly* before the eyes of men.
But all will be in readiness, so that if the Adversary
should again be free from his imprisonment, sin would
be aroused at once, and the whole world again would
lie in wickedness. Thus sin and sinners would speedily
assume their old position, and peace would have pro-
minence no more, except it should please God to pour

forth an amount of His constraining grace which hitherto has not been granted to the world.

We are told in the *twentieth chapter* of REVELATION, that "when the thousand years are expired, Satan shall be loosed out of prison, and shall go out to deceive the nations." So, then, it shall be. As, for want of any explanation being granted in the Inspired Word, we did not pause to ask what was meant by Satan being bound and cast into the bottomless pit; so, for the same reason, we will not stay to make inquiry as to his release therefrom. Let it suffice; he shall again walk to and fro in this world, seeking whom he may *sift* and whom he may *devour*. The "LIAR," the "ACCUSER," the ": DECEIVER," still, he will quickly prove himself to be. To overthrow the kingdom of the Lord, to engulf the souls of men in everlasting ruin, to spread sin and misery around, will be, as they have ever been, the base of his designs. So he "shall go out to deceive the nations," and, as in all former time, he shall too well succeed.

What period will be allowed for this renewed attempt against the Lord's dominion is not stated, but from the particulars which are given of the work of evil to be carried on, there is good reason to believe it will be *brief*.

Let us now carefully examine what is said concerning the work which Satan will be permitted to perform.

Two verses only of the chapter to which we just

referred (the twentieth of REVELATION) have described it. They tell us that Satan "shall go out to deceive the nations which are in the four quarters of the earth, Gog and Magog, to gather them together to battle: the number of whom is as the sand of the sea. And they went up on the breadth of the earth, and compassed the camp of the Saints about, and the beloved city." It certainly appears by this that Satan will put forth much energy; and that he and his legions will be *everywhere* at work. The expression "the four quarters of the earth," appears to leave no land excepted: but to intimate that wheresoever there are people to be tempted, there the tempter's hand will be outstretched.

From the chapter now under consideration, we can obtain very little distinct information as to the extent or power of the last outbreak. But this is not the only place in Scripture in which this last display of sin is spoken of. We find it brought forward also, and far more explicitly by EZEKIEL. This prophet—having spoken, in the *thirty-seventh* chapter, of the restoration of Israel, and of the blessings of the reign of David under the new covenant of peace, on which we dwelt particularly in our last lecture—introduces a new subject in the *thirty-eighth* chapter, a subject quite inconsistent with the reign of quietness and holy calm which is to mark that happy age. It reads as follows :—The word of the Lord came unto me, saying, Son of man, set thy face against GOG, the land of MAGOG, the chief Prince of Meshech and Tubal, and prophesy against him, and say, Thus saith the Lord God, Behold, I am against thee, O Gog, the Chief Prince of Meshech and Tubal: and I will turn thee back, and put hooks into thy jaws, and I will bring thee forth, and all thine army, horses, and horsemen, all of them clothed with all sorts of armour, even a great company with bucklers and shields, all of them handling swords: PERSIA, ETHIOPIA, and LIBYA with them: all of them with shield and helmet: GOMER, and all his band; the house of TOGARMAH of the NORTH QUARTERS, and all his bands; and many people with thee. Be thou prepared, and prepare for thyself, thou, and all thy company that are assembled unto thee, and be thou a guard unto them. *After many days thou shalt be visited:* IN THE LATTER YEARS *thou shalt come into the land that is brought back from the sword, and is gathered out of many people, against the mountains of Israel,* which have been always waste: BUT IT IS BROUGHT FORTH OUT OF THE NATIONS, AND THEY SHALL DWELL SAFELY ALL OF THEM. Thou shalt ascend and come like a storm; thou shalt be like a cloud to cover the land, thou and all thy bands, and many people with thee. Thus saith the Lord God, It shall also come to pass, that at the same time shall things come into thy mind,

and thou shalt think an evil thought: and thou shalt
say, *I will go up to the land of unwalled villages; I will go
to them that are at rest, that dwell safely, all of them
dwelling without walls, and having neither bars nor gates,*
to take a spoil, and to take a prey; to turn thine hand
upon the desolate places that are now inhabited, and
upon the people that are gathered out of the nations,
which have gotten cattle and goods, that dwell in the
midst of the land. SHEBA and DEDAN, and the MER-
CHANTS OF TARSHISH, with all the young lions thereof,
shall say unto thee, Art thou come to take a spoil?
Hast thou gathered thy company to take a prey, to
carry away silver and gold, to take away cattle and
goods, to take a great spoil? Therefore, son of man,
prophesy and say unto GOG, Thus saith the Lord God,
In that day, when My people of Israel dwelleth safely,
shalt thou not know it? And thou shalt come from
thy place *out of the north parts,* thou, and many people
with thee, all of them riding upon horses, a great
company, and a mighty army: and thou shalt come up
against My people of Israel as a cloud to cover the land;
it shall be in the latter days."

In this passage, which I have quoted at length, we
find ISRAEL dwelling *securely* in "unwalled villages,"
having "neither bars nor gates." Israel, thus secure,
is spoken of as "brought back from the sword, and

gathered out of many people." It would appear also
that certain nations will be associated in close friendship
with Israel, when Gog shall stand up against them.
Amongst these are mentioned SHEBA, DEDAN, and
TARSHISH. In league with Gog, against God's people,
will be PERSIA, ETHIOPIA, LIBYA, GOMER, and To-
GARMAH. That is to say, when the power of Satan is
again allowed to be exerted over the minds of men, very
few by comparison will stand firmly on the Lord's side,
even though there be in Israel the clearest evidence
that He is King indeed, and though His manifested
power and justice are beyond the reach of question.
Let us examine this, that we may learn something, if
it may be, of the power which Gog will be permitted
to exercise in the world, as well as of the standing
which Israel will take, and the success they will meet
with, when the land shall be besieged by the last
overwhelming army.

We will speak first of ISRAEL and THEIR ALLIES in
the day of the great siege.

I need not call your attention again to the territory
which Israel will possess: that great peninsula,[1] with
its arid deserts rejoicing and blossoming as the rose,
its howling wilderness turned into so many fruitful fields,
its people happy in a "quietness and assurance" which

[1] See Chapter III.

the experience of a thousand years will have taught them to regard as their unceasing portion. But of the nations which are named as Israel's allies we may do well to speak particularly. Referring to the passage we have quoted from EZEKIEL, we find that these allies of the Lord's people will be *three*,—SHEBA, DEDAN, and TARSHISH.

SHEBA, which is the first mentioned, is said by Josephus to be "Egypt and Ethiopia."[1] But there are good reasons for considering Josephus to have been mistaken: though it is possible (and the annals of Ethiopia, referred to by Bruce, confirm it) that the famous Queen of Sheba had dominions in that country. Indeed our Saviour says that this Queen was "the Queen of the SOUTH," and "came from THE UTTERMOST PARTS OF THE EARTH." Now this might be properly asserted if she came from the *Arabian* banks of the Red Sea,—but *not* if she came from *Ethiopia*,—as a reference to a map will show plainly. Moreover, there is reason for supposing that, although (according to Major Scott Phillips and others) a considerable tract of land on the east of the Red Sea, about one thousand miles in length by an average of three hundred wide, will not be appropriated to any of the tribes of Israel, yet that it will be occupied by nations subject to the King of Israel's

---

[1] *Antiquities.* Book VIII. c. vi. § 5.

sovereignty. *Border States ministering to the wants of the twelve tribes.* There, perhaps, KEDAR will be in readiness to supply servants.[1] There NEBAIOTH will make folds for flocks.[2] There SEBA will cultivate her land, and reap abundance, that she may offer gifts.[3] And there SHEBA, too, having the *" South "* lands, will dig her mines, and heap her stores of gold, and gather incense for the Temple of a greater King than he whose wisdom in the days of old amazed her Queen.[4]

The second place mentioned is DEDAN. This seems to be a tract of land about five hundred miles in length, and of uncertain width (probably about one hundred miles), occupying the extremity of the land of Arabia, having the Persian Gulf on the north-west and north-east; a country well-fitted for the occupation of those who should serve Israel with the merchandise of India.

Then as to TARSHISH.—" The *Merchants* " thereof only are spoken of. Hence we may at once conclude that wherever Tarshish may be situated it is a *mercantile country*. But of what country *at the present time* are merchants in such proximity to Arabia (the future land of Israel) as to warrant our reference to *them*, as the men who (supposing their mercantile character to continue) will rise up and stand by God's people when

---

[1] Isa. lx. 7.   [2] Isa. lx. 7.   [3] Ps. lxxii. 10.   [4] Isa. lx. 6.

P

they shall be suddenly besieged by Satan's multitudes?
I think our eyes will either pass immediately across the
sea *eastward* from DEDAN till we arrive at India; or
they will look *northward* to the shores of "THE GREAT
SEA"—the MEDITERRANEAN. But, in either case,
the sought-for *merchants* which would more especially
attract attention from all nations in the days in which
we live, are those pertaining to the people of GREAT
BRITAIN, for these are they who may be called with
faithful emphasis *The Merchants of India* and *The
Merchants of the Mediterranean.* But the people of
Great Britain possess the famous GIBRALTAR,—"the
key of the Mediterranean:" at, or close to which
important stronghold (not farther, certainly, than Cadiz
on the west, or Malaga on the east) was the famous
TARTESSUS of the ancients, which, as almost all commentators are agreed, was the TARSHISH of Scripture,
associated so constantly and closely with "The Isles."[1]

OUR OWN DEAR ENGLAND, then (there is some ground
to *hope*), may be a nation which God has prepared to
stand by those who are, by a peculiar choice, HIS
PEOPLE, even to the last.

Another matter adds strength to this most acceptable
ground of hope. England is said to have been twice
colonized by the descendants of TARSHISH, the son of

[1] Ps. lxxii. 10; Isa. xxiii. 1, 2, 6; lx. 9, etc.

Javan; viz., by the Tyrians and the Carthaginians, agreeably indeed to the declaration—" And the Sons of Javan ; Elishah, Tarshish, Kittim, and Dodanim. By these were the Isles of the Gentiles divided."[1] A declaration which may fairly be viewed as a prophecy.

When, therefore, "THE MERCHANTS OF TARSHISH" are spoken of, will it be considered that we form an opinion foolishly, if we suppose that the people of our own beloved country, who, for purposes of trade, inhabit our Indian Colonies, may be intended ? Or shall we be thought to reason groundlessly if we argue favourably with regard to THE STABILITY OF OUR BRITISH EMPIRE, EVEN WHEN SO MANY NATIONS OF THE EARTH WILL BE SHAKEN TO THEIR EVERLASTING OVERTHROW ?

But if there be indeed a basis for an expectation so happy, let our Christian fellow-countrymen remember also that TARSHISH is to be *severely chastened* (although not destroyed) before the dawn of the Millennial peace.[2] God will chastise her with a rod of bitterness; but from the burden of her chastisement she will arise and shine in glory, and be well prepared to stand in all the greatness of her strength, when, in the latest hour of this world's evening, INIQUITY BREAKS FORTH WITH SUCH EXCEEDING MIGHT.

Thus far, then, for the nations which in the last

[1] Gen. x. 4, 5.   .   [2] Isa. ii. 16; xxiii. 1, 6.

outburst of evil shall stand firmly as *the friends of Israel.*

Let us now observe also the *other* nations, which will gather round the banner of the deceived monarch GOG. They are PERSIA, ETHIOPIA, LIBYA, GOMER, and TOGARMAH.

As to PERSIA, we need only point to any map of Asia, and call to mind the capabilities which that vast country once displayed, and may display again, for attaining power and greatness.

ETHIOPIA, if we are to comprehend beneath that name the whole of the "Ethiopia Interior" of the ancients, will reach from East to West of Africa, having the "Mountains of the Moon" on the South.

LIBYA, also, if we are to include "Libya" proper, "Libya Deserta," and "Libya Interior," stretches from Egypt, north of "Ethiopia Interior," to the extreme west.

The situation and extent of GOMER are not so easily determined. GOMER was the eldest son of Japheth.[1] It is said that his descendants peopled a considerable part of Asia Minor. From thence they emigrated, till Germany, Gaul, and perhaps some portions of more northerly countries, were occupied by them. In fact, it is supposed that the Cimmerii, Cimbri, Cumbri, Umbri, Cambri, and others, were but names of different

[1] Gen. x. 2.

tribes of Gomer, which spread themselves from the Black Sea to the Atlantic, and from the shores of the Baltic to Italy; the additional names of Celts, Gauls, Galatæ, and Gaels, being given to them.[1] Whether this be correct or not, thus far appears probable, that the descendants of Gomer *did* spread themselves over a great part of Southern Europe, including FRANCE and GERMANY. It seems, then, that in GOMER we have the representative of all the great European powers—England, perhaps, excepted—united in support of GOG.

But what of TOGARMAH? He was the third son of GOMER.[2] The opinion prevails that the children of TOGARMAH peopled the regions of Armenia, Cappadocia, and Phrygia.

If, then, these explanations be correct, and we combine Persia, Ethiopia, Libya, Gomer, and Togarmah, what a *vast strength* we find prepared to side with GOG! From India to the West of Europe, and from the Mountains of the Moon, perhaps, even to the Baltic, shall these apostatizing nations be which will take part against the people of the Lord.

But concerning the important personages, GOG and MAGOG.

The thirty-eighth chapter of EZEKIEL speaks thus:—"And the word of the Lord came unto me, saying,

---

[1] See Calmet.   [2] Gen. x. 3.

Son of man, set thy face against Gog, the land of
Magog, the chief prince of Meshech and Tubal, and
prophesy against him; and say, Thus saith the Lord
God, Behold I am against thee, O Gog, the chief prince
of Meshech and Tubal." The meaning of this passage,
as it stands thus, is by no means evident. But perhaps
we can throw a little light upon it by reference to the
Septuagint translation, where it stands as follows:—
" Και εγενετο λογοs Κυριου προs με . . . στηρισον το προσωπον
σου επι Γωγ, και την γην του Μαγωγ, αρχοντα, 'Ρωs, Μεσοχ,
και Θοβελ, . . . και ειπον αυτω . . . ιδου εγω επι σε αρχοντα
'Ρωs, Μεσοχ, και Θοβελ;" which in English would read
thus:—"And a word of the Lord came unto me . . . set
thy face against Gog and the land of Magog, Prince
of Rhos, Mesoch, and Thobel, . . . and say to him . . .
Behold I (am) against thee, Prince of Rhos, Mesoch,
and Thobel." Now, if this rendering be received,
and Gog, inhabiting the land of Magog, be the Prince
of Rhos, Mesoch, and Thobel,[1] there is but little difficulty in arriving at a conclusion probably correct.

Magog, a son of Japheth, is generally believed to
have been the father of the Scythians and Tartars;
and the Tartars and Muscovites possess the territories

---

[1] That Gog, not Magog, is the prince of Rosh, Mesoch, and Thobel, is
proved by reference to chapter xxxix. 1, where we read, " Behold I am
against thee, O Gog, the chief prince (or rather the prince of Rosh) of
Meshech and Tubal."

which belonged in ancient time to the SCYTHIANS, and retain several traces of the names "GOG and MAGOG." [1] Therefore we may deem it at least probable that Gog the prince of Rosh (ראש), or Rhos ('Ρως), is, in fact, the prince who shall have sway in that vast country we call RUSSIA. Nay, this surely becomes almost more than probability, when we couple Mesech (or Mesoch) and Tubal (or Thobel) with Rosh (or Rhos); for if we bear in mind that *ou* and *sk* are terminations peculiar to the Sclavonic languages, we find MESOCH and THOBEL more nearly allied than perhaps we had expected to MOSCOW and TOBOLSK. Now RUSSIA, MOSCOW, and TOBOLSK were in old time the three divisions of the RUSSIAN EMPIRE. Who, then, is more likely to be the GOG here spoken of, than he who, in the last hour of this earth's eventide, shall have dominion over RUSSIA? And what country is more likely than RUSSIA—*the Scythians' land*—to prove itself "THE LAND OF MAGOG"?

So, then, we have shown, that the nations which shall be confederate against Israel at the time of which we speak, will be many, great, and powerful. And those who still adhere to her as firm allies will be but *few*, and for the more part *weak*;—TARSHISH being the only great and independent nation spoken of, and of Tarshish the whole people not being brought forward,

----

[1] See Calmet.

but "the merchants" and "the young lions" thereof only.

Thus, when Satan shall be loosed out of his prison, he will go out to deceive the nations; and with a *vast multitude* of people he will have success. And these, led on by Gog—whom Satan will empower as he did Antichrist a thousand years before—will "think an evil thought;" and will come up "to take a spoil and to take a prey" from the land of riches and of peace.

Now, it is declared, in the brief prophecy of this outbreak, in the twentieth chapter of the Revelation, that the nations "went up on the breadth of the earth, and compassed the camp of the saints round about, and the beloved city." This passage brings us to the point at which the armies are assembled on the eve of carrying out the grand object of their union. All things are ready: the munitions of war are complete; and the armies of the wicked nations are prepared to go up "*on the breadth of the earth.*" It does not at first sight appear at all evident what is intended by this expression, "*the breadth of the earth.*" It may be worthy of examination. It stands thus in the original—"$\kappa\alpha\iota\ \dot{\alpha}\nu\epsilon\beta\eta\sigma\alpha\nu\ \dot{\epsilon}\pi\iota\ \tau o\ \pi\lambda\alpha\tau o\varsigma\ \tau\eta\varsigma\ \gamma\tilde{\eta}\varsigma$;" which may be translated thus— "*And they mounted upon the broad place of the land.*" Now, undoubtedly, "the land," the possession of which is to be the grand object of this unholy confederacy, is

THE LAND OF ISRAEL.[1] And the particular point of the combined attack is to be JERUSALEM, "THE BELOVED CITY."[2] But in order to besiege Jerusalem, in the situation which it will occupy in the Millennial age, it will be necessary to *mount the height of the exalted plain,* which will reach (as I have endeavoured to show in my last chapter) from Geba to Rimmon, and from the Mediterranean to the Dead Sea; that is to say, about *sixty miles square.* This I conceive to be *" the breadth of the earth,"* or *" the broad place of the land,"* on which it is declared they shall *" go up."* Here, no doubt, the mighty armies of the confederate nations, the allies of GOG, will be assembled, that they may lay siege against *"* the camp of the saints, and the beloved city."

And now that they have prepared all for the attack, and "Sheba, Dedan, and the merchants of Tarshish, with all the young lions thereof," have uttered their remonstrance—"Art thou come to take a spoil? hast thou gathered thy company to take a prey, to carry away silver and gold, to take away cattle and goods, to take a great spoil?"—then it will be immediately the work of GOD HIMSELF to stand up on behalf of Israel. There will be no battle fought; no scaling engine will be raised; no sword effectually drawn against the servants of the Lord; but He will raise His own Almighty

[1] Ezek. xxxviii.   [2] Rev. xx. 9.

arm, and He will work, and none shall let it. So, when
it is declared in the brief record given us in the Book
of REVELATION—"And they went up on the breadth
of the earth, and compassed the Camp of the Saints
about, and the beloved City;" we find this further
declaration,—"AND FIRE CAME DOWN FROM GOD OUT
OF HEAVEN, AND DEVOURED THEM."

But we shall again find details in the thirty-eighth
chapter of EZEKIEL, commencing with the eighteenth
verse,—"And it shall come to pass at the same time
when GOG shall come against the land of Israel, saith
the Lord God, that My fury shall come up in My face.
For in My jealousy, and in the fire of My wrath, have
I spoken, Surely in that day there shall be a great
shaking in the land of Israel; so that the fishes of the
sea, and the fowls of heaven, and the beasts of the
field, and all creeping things that creep upon the earth,
and all the men that are upon the face of the earth,
shall shake *at My Presence;* and the mountains shall be
thrown down, and the steep places shall fall, and every
wall shall fall to the ground. And I will call for a
sword against him throughout all My mountains, saith
the Lord God: *every man's sword shall be against his
brother. And I will plead against him with pestilence and
with blood; and I will reign upon him, and upon his
bands, and upon the many people that are with him,*

an overflowing rain, and great hailstones, fire, and brimstone."[1]

It seems, then, that when the nations are assembled on the great plain of Jerusalem, compassing the city round about for an immediate attack,—THE LORD SHALL APPEAR as the defender of His people: fear and trembling will fall upon the nations: the sword of Israel will be called for: and in the confederate camp there will be slaughter, brother against brother, as in the days of Gideon and of Jonathan. Moreover, the Lord will plead with PESTILENCE; like that, perhaps, which is described by ZECHARIAH—"Their flesh shall consume away while they stand upon their feet, and their eyes shall consume away in their holes, and their tongue shall consume away in their mouth. . . . . And so shall be the plague of the horse, of the mule, of the camel, and of the ass, and of all the beasts that shall be in their tent, as this plague."[2] And He will also plead with *blood;* for the slaughter shall be very great, because "it shall come to pass in that day that a great

---

[1] It may be right to note that it appears to me that with this 38th chapter of Ezekiel the most distant point in the prophecy is arrived at. The next chapter still deals with Gog and Magog, but commences a fresh prophecy concerning them, having for its period of fulfilment the time immediately *preceding* the restoration of Israel and the erection of the Millennial Temple. A careful perusal of the 39th chapter will, I think, place this beyond doubt. [2] Zech. xiv. 12–15.

tumult from the Lord shall be among them; and they shall lay hold every one on the hand of his neighbour, and his hand shall rise up against the hand of his neighbour. And Judah also shall fight at Jerusalem."[1] Nor is this all; for the Lord will plead with *fire;* He will rain upon Gog and upon his bands, and upon the many people that are with him, great hailstones, fire and brimstone; yea, fire shall come down from God out of heaven, and devour them.

So shall the last outbreak of iniquity be silenced, and its power destroyed. It would appear that no *effectual* blow will be struck against God's people. He whom they have served will keep them safely, and not a hair of their head shall perish.

Thus the time will have arrived, not only for the punishment of *sinners,* but also for the effectual rooting out of *sin.* And so we read that the DEVIL, that deceived the nations, will be "cast into the *lake of fire and brimstone,* where the BEAST and the FALSE PROPHET are, and shall be tormented day and night for ever and ever."[2] He is not *now* to be bound in prison for a certain period, whence again he may go forth and re-commence his work of evil, but he is to be cast into *Hell, into the fire that never shall be quenched,* that there,

---

[1] Compare Ezek. xxxviii. 21, with Zech. xiv. 13, 14.

[2] Rev. xx. 10.

in torment, day and night, he may, beyond the reach of any whom he might excite to sin, endure for all eternity the fearful penalty his works deserve.

Thus SATAN—the great prince of darkness—the author of man's sin and misery—who in all ages of the world has laboured to uproot the work of God, and to eradicate all virtue, and all peace, and to overthrow eternally the kingdom of the Lord of lords—will pass from the presence of God's children, leaving HIM, "WHOSE RIGHT IT IS," to reign in undisturbed possession; leaving ISRAEL in peace; leaving EVERY SAINT unscathed; *not having taken one believing, praying soul of man, since Adam fell, from the protecting arm of God;* nay, leaving vividly on record, that the praises of the everlasting age may dwell upon it in the blissful harmony of Heaven, "WHERE SIN ABOUNDED, GRACE DID MUCH MORE ABOUND: THAT AS SIN HATH REIGNED UNTO DEATH, EVEN SO MIGHT GRACE REIGN, THROUGH RIGHTEOUSNESS, UNTO ETERNAL LIFE, BY JESUS CHRIST OUR LORD."

CHAPTER VIII.

The Last Resurrection and Judgment.

———◦○◦———

" Out of Zion, the perfection of beauty, God hath shined. Our God shall
come, and shall not keep silence : a fire shall devour before Him, and it
shall be very tempestuous round about Him. He shall call to the
heavens from above, and to the earth, that He may judge His
people."   PSALM l. 2–4.

———◦○◦———

WE have already dwelt upon the probability that
THE LAST OUTBREAK OF WICKEDNESS will be
very brief; its fury being cut short by the
tremendous stroke of the Almighty arm. But the
crowning effort of the Wicked One being thus turned
into foolishness, all things will be ready for that awful
and amazing scene which is to close this earth's eventful
eventide, and introduce again the darkness which in the
primæval days dwelt " on the face of the deep."

That ONE REMAINING SCENE is now to come before us
for consideration.

Not every eye will feast upon the glories of the Reign
of Peace, nor behold the tabernacle of the Lord with
men. Not every heart will swell with rapture at the
blessedness of the Millennial inheritance, nor join the

praises which from multitudes out of all nations will ascend acceptably to the Eternal Father's throne. But now that the Millennial Reign is passed, and Satan is secured in the eternal prison-house, whence there is no return, the day is come for God Almighty to be "All in All."[1] AN EVERLASTING END MUST BE PUT ONCE FOR ALL TO SIN, AND THE DESERTS OF EVERY MAN AND EVERY DEVIL EVERLASTINGLY AWARDED. *Every eye*, therefore, must now behold, and *every heart* be aroused to confidence or dread.

For this the voice of THE ETERNAL SON OF GOD shall be uttered with almighty strength; the vast depths of earth and sea shall be penetrated; the continents and isles attend; and "in a moment, in the twinkling of an eye," WILL ALL THE DEAD GIVE HEED,—the dead of yesterday; the dead of ages past; their ashes for whom the tears have just begun to flow, and theirs whose names have for revolving centuries been buried in oblivion. All these shall hear, and heed, and rise; their old corruption put on incorruption, and their mortal immortality, Before the call of the Almighty Voice, their bodies will abide as silently as ever, in the earth or ocean depths, enshrined securely and at rest; but when that Voice shall have poured forth its word, it will be otherwise. But now the surface of the earth and sea will be covered

[1] 1 Cor. xv. 28.

quickly with a multitude no man can number—the dead, both saved, and lost from the Millennial age, and those who in all ages and all nations have departed, *but are not in Christ*,—these shall come forth incorruptible, and stand prepared for judgment.

It would appear that when these have arisen, EARTH itself, untenanted by the remains of any son of Adam, will receive its portion of the judgment, for the sin with which, since the primæval fall, it has been stained.

Raised high, in the sight of all, will be the GREAT WHITE THRONE; and on the seat thereof, the SON OF MAN, arrayed in the eternal glory of the Father, will hold session. From the brightness of His face all nature will shrink back. The heaven and the earth will flee away, and no place be found for them.[1] The judgment of Almighty God will be visited upon them, and they must pay the penalty of sin, according to the word of prophecy,—" The heavens shall pass away with a great noise, and the elements shall melt with fervent heat; the earth also, and the works that are therein, shall be burned up; . . . . the heavens being on fire shall be dissolved, and the elements shall melt with fervent heat."[2] *How* this shall be, we know not. That it *will be*, is certain, as the Word of God is true. But when the earth, and heavens which

---

[1] Rev. xx. 11.   [2] 2 Pet. iii. 10-12.

surround the earth, have passed away in fire from the exceeding glory of the King of kings,—"the dead both small and great" are to be summoned to the Throne: and will obey. It is not to be now, as on a former day, that the Lord will send His angels to gather His Elect from the four winds, from one end of *Heaven* to the other;—but that He will send them to call forth the Saints departed in the course of the Millennial Reign of Peace, and to constrain the multitudes of the *unsaved*, who have risen from the tomb, the grave, the sea, that they ascend and gather round *the Great White Throne*, that He who sits thereon may bring their deeds to light, and judge them in His righteousness. From this assembly not one soul of all the risen dead will be excepted.

But here I pause an instant, lest among my readers there be any who have lived regardless of their day of grace. Oh, let me speak a faithful word to them. It is a very little while, before both you and I must leave this world that we may stand before the Lord. As the tree falls, so it must lie. As we die, so we must abide until the day of resurrection. God gives us all a day of grace, wherein are ample opportunities granted us for turning to Him, and obtaining sure acceptance. No one of us can stand up against God, and say that opportunities have been denied him; for Christ Jesus

Q

has made full atonement for the sins *of all*, and to believe in Him is to be *justified* and *saved*. I would ask each of my readers to weigh carefully the following passages, and then to ask himself,—CAN I ESCAPE IF I NEGLECT SO GREAT SALVATION?

JESUS said, "As Moses lifted up the serpent in the wilderness, even so must the SON OF MAN be lifted up, that WHOSOEVER BELIEVETH ON HIM SHOULD NOT PERISH, BUT HAVE EVERLASTING LIFE."[1]

Jesus said again, "VERILY, VERILY, I SAY UNTO YOU, HE THAT BELIEVETH ON ME HATH EVERLASTING LIFE."[2]

Is not the way of our salvation plain? Need any sinner perish? Need an anxious, burdened soul go on his way unpardoned? *As* the serpent-bitten children of Israel did but LOOK upon the brazen image Moses reared, and received healing *instantly*, however deep the wound, however far the deathly venom had penetrated the system; *so* may the conscience-stricken sinner, who is bitten by the Serpent which deceived Eve, and in whose soul the poison of iniquity has been effecting its sure work of death, look up to Jesus Christ,—look up to Him with simple trust, and live. No burdened soul which looks on Him with faith *can* perish. The weakest of believers on the Son of God shall have a glorious, never-

---

[1] John iii. 14, 15. Read also verses 16–18, and 36.

[2] John vi. 47. See also Acts xvi. 31 ; Rom. v. 1, and x. 8, 9, etc.

failing portion in the Saints' inheritance. WHO, THEN,
SHALL ESCAPE IF HE NEGLECT SO GREAT SALVATION,
ATTAINABLE, MOREOVER, BY SUCH VERY SIMPLE MEANS?

To return.   Let us observe more carefully the attitude
which the SAVED OF THE LORD shall be privileged to
assume.   All these shall be gathered.   Already they
have known the King, for they have shared with Him
the government of the Millennial Kingdom, or else have
been therein His earthly subjects.   They have known
that they are saved.'   They have known that condemnation cannot be the portion of the weakest soul among
them. But still they must stand there for *judgment*.[1] And
a strict all-searching scrutiny they must bear.   They
have built, indeed, by grace, on *the foundation God has
laid*, and *they are safe*, though heaven and earth shall
pass away.   *Some* of them have built with gold, some
with silver, some with precious stones, on this foundation.
Each of these will stand the test of the devouring flame
with greater or less firmness.   *Others* have built only
with wood, or hay, or stubble, which that devouring flame
will speedily consume.   As these redeemed ones stand
there before the Lord, the fire of His all-searching
justice will effectually try the work of every man, *to prove
it, of what sort it is;* and if, thus being tested by the
fire, the work of any man abide which he has built, *he*

[1] Rom. xiv. 10–12 ; 2 Cor. v. 10 ; Rev. xx. 11-15.

shall receive reward accordingly. But if any man's work be burned, he shall *suffer loss :* yet " HE HIMSELF SHALL BE SAVED ; " although it may be *just* saved—" so as by fire." [1]

Thus, then, without a fear of condemnation, yet awaiting an unerring sentence, according to the rightful measure of God's approbation, will the Righteous stand before the Judge of all.

One word on their condition. We have called them " RIGHTEOUS." Truly so : for "*righteous*" is their fitting title. Christ Himself has called them by this name.[2]

Shall I be thought to assert that which *is not,* if I say that the very weakest of believers,—though his life may have been *vile with sin* before he came to Christ with faith,—is already *perfectly righteous* before God? From that moment in which he believed in Jesus Christ, and trusted his immortal soul implicitly to Him, he is not only *forgiven,* not only *saved,* but he is ACTUALLY RIGHTEOUS in the sight of Heaven. But an assertion such as this must not be allowed to pass unproved. Let us inquire concerning it in the Word of God. The grand truths which are so patent in the Bible, viz., that the Lord hath laid on Christ the iniquity of us all ; that Christ hath taken our place, borne our sins and endured their punishment, so that by His stripes we are healed ;

[1] 1 Cor. iii. 11-15.   [2] Matt. xiii. 43 ; xxv. 46.

are comforting indeed to the sincere believer.   But they form a *part* only of the great treasure which God's hand holds forth for the acceptance of the anxious soul.   The believer in Christ Jesus is not only washed in His atoning blood: he is not only rendered clean, the guilt and filthiness of his transgressions being taken from him; but he is *justified* also; he is *clothed upon*, as it were, with RIGHTEOUSNESS which is *not his own*, nor has been wrought by any *creature* in the universe; even the RIGHTEOUSNESS OF GOD, IN CHRIST.[1]   See, how unmistakably the Apostle Paul dwells upon this in the third chapter of his Epistle to the ROMANS.   Having declared the fact that "All the world" is "guilty before God," and that "By the deeds of the law there shall no flesh be justified in His sight;" he adds— "But now THE RIGHTEOUSNESS OF GOD *without the law* is manifested, being witnessed by the law and the prophets: even THE RIGHTEOUSNESS OF GOD WHICH IS BY FAITH OF JESUS CHRIST, UNTO ALL AND UPON ALL THEM THAT BELIEVE: for there is no difference: for all have sinned and come short of the glory of God; being justified freely by His grace through the redemption that is in Christ Jesus."   What is it, then, but that, *in the very highest sense*, believers in the Son of God are entitled to be called "RIGHTEOUS"—and

---

[1] Jer. xxiii. 6 ; Rom. iii. 21-26 ; 1 Cor. i. 30, 31 ; 2 Cor. v. 21, etc.

that the richest blessings of the Righteous must be *theirs,* for they, being cleansed from all this guilt in the precious blood of Christ, are clothed in the very RIGHTEOUSNESS OF GOD! I cannot help referring on this subject to a passage in the writings of "the judicious Hooker," which speaks very powerfully and with great fulness to the point. He says, "Although in ourselves we be altogether sinful and unrighteous, yet even the man which in himself is impious, full of iniquity, full of sin; him *being found in Christ through faith, and having his sins in hatred through repentance:* him God beholdeth with a gracious eye, putteth away his sin by not imputing it, taking quite away the punishment due thereunto by pardoning it; and accepteth him in Jesus Christ, as perfectly righteous, as if he had fulfilled all that is commanded him in the law; *shall I say* MORE PERFECTLY RIGHTEOUS *than if himself had fulfilled the whole law?* I must take heed what I say; but *the Apostle* saith,[1] 'God made Him, which knew no sin, *to be sin* for us; that we might be made THE RIGHTEOUSNESS OF GOD in Him.' SUCH WE ARE IN THE SIGHT OF GOD THE FATHER, AS IS THE VERY SON OF GOD HIMSELF. Let it be counted folly, or frenzy, or fury, or whatsoever. It is our wisdom, and our comfort; we care for no knowledge in the

[1] 2 Cor. v. 21.

world but this, that man hath sinned, and God hath suffered; that GOD HATH MADE HIMSELF THE SIN OF MEN, AND MEN ARE MADE THE RIGHTEOUSNESS OF GOD."

This surely is conclusive. For here we have not Hooker's own peculiar opinion given us, but the simple, unmistakable assertion of the WORD OF GOD. And we may conclude that all the multitudes of true believers in the Lord Jesus Christ, whether they have passed the stream of death or not, are RIGHTEOUS in the fullest sense. With every one of them is God well pleased; and righteous in the spotless righteousness of their CREATOR, they shall stand awaiting their reward at the right hand of the Almighty Purchaser of their Eternal Bliss. *How* they will shine forth; *how* they will express their joy; *how* they will declare the praises of their great Jehovah-Tsidkenu; we cannot tell. But *this* we know,—they will be LIKE HIM.[1] They will be prepared, in His unsullied righteousness, to reign with Him in an estate more glorious by far than eye of man hath seen, or ear heard, or heart conceived. They shall inherit the kingdom prepared for them from the foundation of the world. They shall go into LIFE ETERNAL.

Let me here speak a word of encouragement to my fellow-believers. *Is it indeed the case* that every one

[1] 1 John iii. 2.

who believes in Jesus Christ is not only crucified with Christ and washed from every stain in His atoning blood, but also has received the righteousness of Christ, which is indeed the very RIGHTEOUSNESS OF GOD Himself? Is this, I say, indeed the case, and yet do so very many of us go with *fearing, trembling, doubting* footsteps through this earthly life towards heaven? Why do we thus fear? Why do we thus suffer clouds and darkness to interpose between the Lord and our immortal souls? Why do we not *lay hold* at once of the most glorious hope which is set before us in the Gospel? True, true indeed, we have a daily, hourly cause to mourn over evil habits, lukewarmness, and inconsistencies; for "the flesh lusteth against the Spirit and the Spirit against the flesh, and these are contrary the one to the other; so that we cannot do the things that we would."[1] But though it is so, and by reason of the law of sin in our members, the very best amongst us are too often brought into a sore subjection; yet we need not cry out in despair, "O wretched man that I am, who shall deliver me from the body of this death?" But rather, looking boldly upwards,—behold Jesus, sitting at the right hand of Power,—our faithful One, —"The Lord our Righteousness;" and realizing our position through His finished work of love, exclaim,—

[1] Gal· v. 17.

"I thank my God, through Jesus Christ our Lord."[1] Oh, how can any true believer find the slightest room for doubt, when it is declared so plainly that he is arrayed in the pure RIGHTEOUSNESS OF THE ALL-HOLY GOD? Reader, DOST THOU BELIEVE ON THE SON OF GOD? Then it is well with thee, for thou art RIGHTEOUS, and in righteousness shalt stand in the great day of Christ.

We will consider next the ACT OF JUDGMENT.

Not much is told us in the Word of God concerning this. Yet quite enough is said to show that it will be a Judgment, wherein *every secret shall be brought to light, every life and every heart laid bare, every thought and every word with accuracy weighed:* that nothing shall escape the searching eye of the OMNISCIENT JUDGE, nor any soul of man be found unjustly dealt with.

OUR SAVIOUR frequently alluded to the Judgment of mankind, that men might live in constant preparation for it. He spoke of it decidedly as an act in which each hidden thing shall be made manifest;[2] in which all men shall give account for every idle word which they have spoken;[3] in which justice shall be done unerringly to every soul of man; he who had received

---

[1] Rom. vii. 12-45.   [2] Matt. x. 26 ; Mark iv. 22, etc.
[3] Matt. xxv. 31-40.

ten talents, five, or one, being dealt with accordingly; much being expected from that man to whom much had been given, and little being required from him to whom had been committed little. Our Saviour spoke also distinctly about REWARDS and PUNISHMENTS. He told His disciples, clearly and repeatedly, that the slightest act of single-hearted service on the part of God's children should receive express reward. The secret prayer, the silent alms-deed, the unobtrusive act of fasting, the cup of cold water given to a disciple, should be returned in an abundant recompense.[1] Moreover, he by whom the hungry should be fed, the naked clothed, the sick or the imprisoned visited, the stranger lodged, should find his deeds recorded with the spirit in which they had been performed, and dealt with in exact accordance.[2] Whereas, neglect of duty towards God, neglect of the just exercise of love towards men, profession of religion without sincerity,[3] should be punished at the hand of the Great King and Judge.

The language of the Apostles likewise was decided. We need not quote from them passage by passage, as all that they have said must be familiar to the Bible reader. It might suffice to state that the ACTS OF THE APOSTLES, the EPISTLES, and the BOOK OF REVELATION, are in perfect harmony, declaring plainly not only that God

---

[1] Matt. vi. 1–18. [2] Matt. xii. 36. [3] Matt. xxv. 25–28, 41–45.

"hath appointed a day, in the which He will judge the world in righteousness, by that man whom He hath ordained,"[1] but also that He will in that day "try every man's work of what sort it is,"[2] and "judge the secrets of men,"[3] so that "every one may receive the things done in his body, according to that he hath done, whether it be good or bad."[4] But perhaps we may not be deemed wearisome if we pause for an instant to consider one of all these harmonizing testimonies separately; namely, that which is afforded in the twentieth chapter of the REVELATION. The words are few, but they draw a wondrous picture of the awful scene by which that last great act of judgment shall be marked. "And I saw a great white Throne, and Him that sat on it, from whose face the earth and the heaven fled away; and there was found no place for them. And I saw the dead, small and great, stand before God; and the books were opened; and another book was opened, which is the book of life; and the dead were judged out of those things which were written in the books *according to their works.* And the SEA gave up the dead which were in it; and DEATH and HELL (or the grave) delivered up the dead which were in them; and they were judged every man *according to their works.* And

---

[1] Acts xvii. 31. [2] 1 Cor. iii. 13–15.
[3] Rom. ii. 16. [4] 2 Cor. v. 10; Gal. vi. 7, 8.

Death and Hell were cast into the lake of fire. This is the second death. And whosoever was not found written in the Book of Life was cast into the lake of fire." Thus far, then, is evident: There will be a formal opening of the "Books" wherein are entered all the good and evil men have wrought while in the body. What these "Books" are we know not. Whether *actual Records*, with the thoughts, words, and actions of mankind, exist to be produced at the appointed hour of Judgment, we know not, nor need we seek to know. Let it suffice that every secret shall be known, that so full justice may be done, and men, both saved and unsaved, may be judged according to their works.

But now "ANOTHER BOOK" is spoken of as being opened afterwards, which is called "THE BOOK OF LIFE."—We may suppose, then, that when the judgment has been passed upon *the works* of every man, according to their actual merits or demerits, as found written in *the various books first opened*, and all the world,—those on the *right* hand and those on the *left*,— are proved guilty before God; "THE BOOK OF LIFE" will be brought forward, wherein *man's works have no place at all*. This Book, we may presume, tells only of the LOVE, POWER, GRACE, ATONEMENT, AND SALVATION of the LORD JESUS CHRIST, and bears upon its pages the beloved names of those who, through the

mighty power of the Eternal Spirit, have been brought
to apprehend their state of condemnation, and have
gone with singleness of heart to the Redeemer's cross.
Through grace they have believed; through grace they
have maintained their heavenward course; and now,
complete in grace, they stand, without a fear at the
right hand of the Eternal Judge. Nothing have they
whereof they should boast: nothing by which any of
them might be found worthy, so far as their own doings
in the flesh have been concerned. The former Books
have proved that every one of them is guilty before
God. Their repentance has found need to be repented
of, their tears have wanted washing, and their washen
tears have needed to be washed again in the blood of
the Redeemer. But *by grace they are what they are,*
pardoned, justified, and saved souls; children of God:
heirs of glorious immortality. "The Book of Life"
contains their names. And their *poor imperfect works do
follow them.* But as to these works which will follow
them—Have they been wrought with singleness of
heart towards God? Have they been done with a
sincere desire to glorify His Word; with fervent
love towards Him; and in sincere brotherhood with
His redeemed people? If so, *in what degree? How
fervent* has been the desire? *How deep* the love? *How
close* the brotherhood? for the eternal crown shall be

accordingly. " As one star differeth from another star in glory, so also is the resurrection of the dead." Although when the works stood *by themselves* for judgment, their actual merits being tested by the former books, they could do nothing but condemn ; yet *now that they stand forth as the efforts* (weak, indeed, and very faulty) *of the heart renewed by the Eternal Spirit's grace,* they are accepted *in Christ Jesus.*

Upon these whose names shall be found written in this Book of Life, the blessings of eternal glory will abide; they shall inherit everlasting happiness; the peace of " NEW JERUSALEM " shall be their portion for the everlasting age. As to their estate of glory in that heavenly city we shall have to speak in our next chapter.

For the present let us be content to note, that every believer in the Lord Jesus, standing on the right hand of the Redeemer's throne, shall find his name recorded in THE LAMB'S BOOK OF LIFE ! And He who shall be seated on the throne will make confession of his name before His Father and the holy angels, and will say to him, " WELL DONE, GOOD AND FAITHFUL SERVANT; ENTER THOU INTO THE JOY OF THY LORD."

But as to those whose names shall *not* be found written in the BOOK OF LIFE,—it is declared that their eternal portion is to be " THE LAKE OF FIRE." They did not confess the Lord while they were yet on earth, and now the Lord will not confess their names before His Father which is in Heaven. They who rejected Him must be themselves rejected. They who dishonoured Him must be themselves dishonoured. They who set at nought His counsel, and would none of His reproof, must "eat the fruit of their own ways, and be filled with their own devices." They will plead, "Lord, have we not eaten and drunk in Thy presence, and hast Thou not taught in our streets? Have we not in Thy name cast out devils, and done many wonderful works?"[1] But their pleading will be all in vain. The door of MERCY will be shut by the stern hand of JUSTICE; and the word of Christ will be, "I never knew you, depart from Me, all ye workers of iniquity," and, as it is elsewhere given, "Depart from Me, ye cursed, into everlasting fire, prepared for the devil and his angels." And they shall go away into everlasting punishment,[2] in the LAKE OF FIRE.

O that the ungodly, the careless, the worldly, and all those who have put off the matters of salvation to a future day, would think whether it is worth their while to live as they are living, when at any moment they may be called hence, and nothing but a fearful looking for of this tremendous sentence must be their portion till that day in which they shall *receive it!* O that they

---

[1] Matt. vii. 22 ; Luke xiii. 26.   [2] Matt. xxv. 46.

would calmly think whether it is not the part of wisdom to break off at once from all iniquity, accept the full salvation freely offered to whosoever will, and give their hearts to God! Forgive me, reader,—"*Who can dwell with devouring flames?* Who will be so great *a fool* as to allow his NEVER-DYING SOUL to glide on smoothly towards so TERRIBLE A CONDEMNATION, when the Great Lord Himself has promised him a full and free salvation, through His own priceless blood and righteousness, if he will come from the unholy paths which worldlings tread, and in sincerity and truth accept it at His hands.

With this dread sentence on the wicked, it appears that the last session of the great Almighty Judge will terminate. And now what further shall prevent the Son of Man *resigning the Millennial Throne?* He has reigned till *all His enemies* have been put beneath His feet, and DEATH has been consigned for ever to the lake of fire. Christ *was* to reign till all this should be done; as it is written,—"*Then* cometh the end, *when* He shall have put down all rule and all authority and power. *For He must reign till He hath put all His enemies under His feet.* THE LAST ENEMY THAT SHALL BE DESTROYED IS DEATH." [1] But, clearly, it is as the SON OF MAN, reigning over the children of Adam *upon the earth*, and in this sense alone, that His reign is then to terminate.

[1] I Cor. xv. 24-26.

Having, *as the Son of Man*, put down and thoroughly subdued all evil principalities, authorities, and powers, and put all enemies—even death—under His feet; He will, *as Son of Man*, deliver up the *earthly* kingdom, wherein these opponents of His reign existed, into the hands of the ETERNAL FATHER. Still He will be King; still He will reign; still, exalted high upon the Throne of Glory, He will sit and rule. The NEW — THE HEAVENLY— JERUSALEM will be the place wherein, among the true and holy ISRAEL redeemed from every nation of the earth, He will delight to manifest His presence and exalt His love.   There shall it be recorded for the everlasting age, that the Redeemer lives and reigns; there, upon the throne of David, although not after any earthly manner, He will sit "to order it and to establish it . . . for ever;" and there shall it be seen that "OF THE INCREASE OF HIS GOVERNMENT AND PEACE THERE SHALL BE NO END."

And thus, although it will be true that "the Son also Himself shall be subject unto Him that put all things under Him, that God may be all in all; "[1] yet will it be only a subjection of the MANHOOD for the magnification of the GODHEAD.   And so the reign of Christ will be as actual *then* and *for the everlasting age*, as when God gave to Him "the heathen for His inheritance, and the uttermost parts of the earth for His possession.

[1] 1 Cor. xv. 27, 28.   R

With this resignation of the earthly kingdom into the Eternal Father's hand will the momentous EVENING OF THE DAY OF JUDGMENT close; upon this will follow instantly (for there will be no night except in Hell) THE DAWN OF THE ETERNAL DAY OF GLORY. Then will be the shout, "Lift up your heads, O ye gates, and be ye lift up, ye everlasting doors; and the King of Glory shall come in." Then will be the blissful welcome from the Hosts who never fell, to the Redeemed from earth; then will "a multitude no man can number, out of all nations, and kindreds, and people and tongues"— gathered, not from the great tribulation only, but from the Millennial period also—stand forth before the throne, and before the Lamb, clothed with white robes, and palms in their hands, and giving heavenly praise for their salvation, render blissful service to the Lord who bought them. Glorious and supremely happy shall their portion be. No care, no cross, no fear, no sin; but blessings, richest blessings, such as eye hath never seen, nor ear heard, nor heart conceived; for in their Father's House shall be their glorious abode, and in His manifested presence they shall offer praise; and "THE LAMB, WHICH IS IN THE MIDST OF THE THRONE, SHALL FEED THEM, AND SHALL LEAD THEM TO LIVING FOUNTAINS OF WATERS; AND GOD SHALL WIPE AWAY ALL TEARS FROM THEIR EYES."

CHAPTER IX.

The New Jerusalem.

"And I, John, saw the holy city, New Jerusalem, coming down from God out of Heaven, prepared as a bride adorned for her husband."

REV. xxi. 2.

THE heaven and the earth shall flee away, from the bright shining of His face who will be seated on the Great White Throne of Judgment. This is a plainly stated fact, on which we need not be ashamed to decline offering comment. No thoughtful person will be disposed to blame us for receiving it as it is placed before us in the language of the inspired St. John, *without remark.*—"I saw," said he, " a Great White Throne, and Him that sat on it, from whose face the earth and the heaven fled away; and there was found no place for them."[1] It is enough for us, that we are again and again forewarned of this amazing fact in Holy Scripture; so that if we receive the testimony of the Word of God *at all*, we cannot but

[1] Rev. xx. 11.

look forward to a time when "Heaven and earth shall pass away."

But an event both great and wonderful will *follow* upon this, concerning which we find much information, and in which we are peculiarly interested: I mean, THE NEW CREATION. "Behold," said He that sat upon the throne to the beloved John—"BEHOLD I MAKE ALL THINGS NEW." [1]

Let us observe, with care, the information which is given us concerning this.

ISAIAH, in the sixty-fifth chapter, in which he also speaks with plainness of the blessings of the Millennial Reign of Peace, carries us beyond it for an instant, saying by the word of the Lord—" The former troubles are forgotten, and . . . . they are hid from mine eyes. For, behold, I CREATE NEW HEAVENS, AND A NEW EARTH: and the former shall not be remembered, nor come into mind. But be ye glad and rejoice for ever in that which I create; for, behold, I create Jerusalem a rejoicing, and her people a joy." Having thus spoken, the Prophet evidently draws back from this glorious new creation, to the *type* of it which is to be afforded by the Millennial period, in which, though curbed exceedingly, both *sin* and *death* will have *their* place.

In the Second Epistle of PETER, the third chapter,

[1] Rev. xxi. 5.

we read as follows: "Seeing then that all these things must be dissolved, what manner of persons ought ye to be in all holy conversation and godliness; looking for, and hasting unto the coming of the Day of God, wherein the heavens being on fire shall be dissolved, and the elements shall melt with fervent heat! Nevertheless we, according to His promise, look for NEW HEAVENS AND A NEW EARTH, wherein dwelleth righteousness. Wherefore, beloved, seeing that ye look for such things, be diligent that ye may be found of Him in peace, without spot and blameless." The Apostle has thus made it very plain, that when, in the great Day of God, the heavens and the earth shall pass away, the Lord will create new heavens and a new earth, which shall be the habitation, not in any wise of those who err, and fall, and sin; but of the righteous who are saved to life eternal.

The most full and clear description which God has afforded us of this in all His Word, we shall find in the twenty-first and twenty-second chapters of the REVELATION. These chapters treat of the NEW HEAVENS and NEW EARTH exclusively.

Beginning with the first verse, we read, "And I saw a NEW HEAVEN and a NEW EARTH: for the first heaven and the first earth were passed away." Here we have the fulfilment, *in vision*, of the prediction which was previously uttered by the Prophets, by our Lord Himself, and by the Apostles. Now in whatever *other* particulars of a physical kind, the NEW EARTH is to differ from the earth of the Millennial period,—there is *one* point which will make a very clear distinction between them. In the Millennial age—the SEA is particularly spoken of, and frequently referred to among the blessings which will be enjoyed by Israel and the nations.[1] But the Apostle John declares pointedly in the description of his vision of the NEW EARTH,—"*And there was no more sea.*" This matter seems to be recorded in order to prevent any risk of confusion in the mind, concerning the Millennial and the *Post*-Millennial earth. The *one* is to have *Sea :* indeed the sea is to be very essential to the well-being of its people ;—the *other* is to have *no Sea* ; none will be needed either for beauty or utility.

Having thus spoken, John continues, "And I saw THE HOLY CITY, NEW JERUSALEM, *coming down from God out of Heaven*, prepared as a bride adorned for her husband. And I heard a great voice out of Heaven, saying, Behold the tabernacle of God is with men, and He will dwell with them, and they shall be His people, and God Himself shall be with them, and be their God. And God shall wipe away all tears from their eyes: and *there shall be no more death*, neither sorrow, nor

[1] See Chapter VI.

crying, neither shall there be any more pain; for the former things are passed away. And He that sat upon the Throne said, BEHOLD I MAKE ALL THINGS NEW. And He said unto me, Write: for these words are true and faithful."

We observe here, that there is no mention of a city to be *built* upon the earth, as in the vision of EZEKIEL: the NEW JERUSALEM is *not to be built,* but it is to come *down out of Heaven* from God. To *come down* to earth, and thereupon abide, its foundations being fixed by God in their appointed place. Earth, made pure by fire, and formed anew, will be prepared by God for all "the nations of them which are saved," and New Jerusalem will be its wonderful Metropolis, the centre of its light, and life, and glory.

Let us follow the Apostle's vision,—to the *construction, dimensions,* and *character* of this NEW JERUSALEM.

As we read the chapter upon which we have been commenting, and also that which follows, we find it recorded that the city is to have "THE GLORY OF GOD," her light being "like unto a stone most precious, even like a jasper stone, clear as crystal." Thus we surely learn that the glory of the Saint's Eternal City will be great indeed. So great, that the city shall have "no need of the sun, neither of the moon, to shine in it." Moreover, by reason of this glory, *day* and *night* will not be recognised. Its wondrous light, which is above the brightness of all light created, will shine forth unceasingly; wherefore it is written, "There shall be no night there: and they shall need no candle, neither light of the sun; for the Lord God shall give them light."[1]

Again: the city is to have "A WALL, great and high;" "TWELVE GATES," guarded by angels of the Lord, and having "the names of the twelve tribes of the Children of Israel" written upon them. Three of these gates are to face the east, three the north, three the south, and three the west; and each of them is to be a pearl. The wall of the city is, moreover, to have "twelve foundations, and in these foundations are to be placed the names of the twelve Apostles of the Lamb." These twelve foundations are to be garnished with all manner of precious stones. The first, jasper; the second, sapphire; the third, chalcedony; the fourth, emerald; the fifth, sardonyx; the sixth, sardius; the seventh, chrysolyte; the eighth, beryl; the ninth, topaz; the tenth, chrysoprasus; the eleventh, jacinth; the twelfth, amethyst. So, indeed, the God of truth has said, to whom the riches of all worlds belong. So,

---

[1] We should be careful to remark that it is not said, the sun shall never shine upon it, but only that by reason of the brighter glory of the Lord, the light of the sun will not be *needed*.

doubtless, therefore, will the everlasting foundations of the New and Heavenly Jerusalem be adorned. The STREET, or rather, the "place" (ἡ πλατεια) of the city is also mentioned. It is to be constructed of "pure gold, as it were transparent glass."

OF SUCH EXCELLENCE AND BEAUTY, O BELIEVER IN THE SON OF GOD, IS THE GREAT CITY OF THINE EVERLASTING HOME. Rejoice then in the prospect, and cast not one wishful look upon the world behind thee. Let "ONWARD, UPWARD, HEAVENWARD, HOMEWARD, LOOKING UNTO JESUS," be thy daily motto; for the GREAT KING hath granted to thy saved soul, A GLORIOUS INTEREST IN THIS BRIGHT JERUSALEM.

Let us observe, there is to be NO TEMPLE in this city. In the *Millennial* Jerusalem, described so minutely by EZEKIEL, there is to be a vast Temple, as we have already seen.[1] But in this NEW JERUSALEM there is to be none. St. John says, "And I saw no Temple therein; for the Lord God Almighty and the Lamb are the Temple of it." But there is to be that which is far better than a Temple, even "THE THRONE OF GOD AND OF THE LAMB;" and that which is far better than the most hallowed of all Temple worship; for it is written that God's "servants shall serve him: and they shall *see His face; and His name shall be written in their foreheads.*"

[1] Chapter v. page 188, etc.

Of what dimensions shall this city be, which is, as it appears, to be the great METROPOLIS of the NEW EARTH? The measurement is given us as follows:— "The city lieth four-square, and *the length is as large as the breadth;* and he (a man with a measuring reed in his hand) measured the city with his reed, TWELVE THOUSAND FURLONGS. The length, and the breadth, and the height of it are equal." Now this at once shows that the dimensions of the city will be *enormous.* Twelve thousand Roman furlongs are equal to ONE THOUSAND FOUR HUNDRED MILES nearly.[1] The city then (having each of its sides one thousand five hundred miles in length) would contain an area not far short of TWO MILLION SQUARE MILES. Its height also— inclusive, of course, of its *foundations,* and, perhaps also, of *internal terraces* rising one above another towards the centre—is to be ONE THOUSAND FOUR HUNDRED MILES. But the Jasper Wall surrounding the city is to be in height "an hundred and forty and four cubits." That is to say (taking twenty-three inches to the cubit), ONE HUNDRED AND SIXTY-SEVEN FEET, the foundations, we may suppose, not being included. The small height of the wall compared with the vast dimensions of the city,

---

[1] Accurately thus. The Roman Stadium, or Furlong, was 625 Roman feet, or 606 feet 9 inches English. Therefore 12,000 stadia, or furlongs, would be about 1,379 English miles.

as well as the apparent absurdity of the idea of a cubical city, will lead at once to the conclusion that the shape must be PYRAMIDAL, towering up from the base of 2, 000,000 square miles, to the street or *place* of gold at the summit, prepared for the throne of God and the Lamb.

It is implied in the most decided manner that the NEW JERUSALEM will descend from Heaven to Earth, and there be fixed for ever, as EARTH'S WONDERFUL METROPOLIS.

In the twenty-first chapter of REVELATION, to which we have been principally referring in this chapter, we find that when John had said of the New Jerusalem, that " the Glory of God did lighten it, and the Lamb is the light thereof," he added " and the *nations* of them which are saved, shall walk in the light of it : and the *kings of the earth* do bring their glory and honour into it. And the gates of it shall not be shut at all by day : for there shall be no night there. And they shall bring *the glory and honour of the nations* into it.

But since it will be thus, we must suppose that when the world is re-constructed, as it were :—when it is made " A NEW EARTH ; "—*its dimensions will be such as to warrant the existence of so extensive* a METROPOLIS. And whence shall an objection to such a change arise ? Cannot He who first formed all things out of nothing, by His word of power *enlarge* a world which He of old *called forth*, if an enlargement should be needed? Most certainly this cannot be a thing *too hard* for the Almighty.

Then *thus* we may believe it *will* be. And on the NEW EARTH, of which the shining capital will be this NEW JERUSALEM, the saved people of the *former* earth will live and glorify the Lord their God, for ever and for ever. The Lord will have His Throne amongst them, "and they shall see His face, and His name shall be in their foreheads, ... and they shall reign for ever and ever." And from the throne of God and of the Lamb, a pure RIVER OF WATER OF LIFE shall flow,[1] and "in the midst of the street of it, and on either side of the river," will be found "THE TREE OF LIFE," bearing "twelve manner of fruits," and yielding her fruit "every month:" and the leaves of the tree will be for the *service*[2] (εἰς θεραπειαν) of the nations. "And there shall be no more curse."

Now what was Eden's beauty,—what Eden's excellence,—compared with that which shall be, when, in the eyes of the adoring "multitude no man can number," the brightness of the New Jerusalem shall be revealed? Truly "eye hath not seen, nor ear heard, neither have entered into the heart of man, the

---

[1] Rev. xxii. 1.　　　[2] Not necessarily "healing," as in our Version.

things which God hath prepared for them that love Him."

We have, I think, seen clearly that the City described so minutely by EZEKIEL, upon the construction and situation of which we dwelt at some length in a former lecture, cannot possibly be the New Jerusalem described in the Apocalypse. The points of difference are as marked as those, on which we commented, between the *Millenial* and the *New* Earth. Amongst the more prominent, we cannot fail to have observed the following: THE JERUSALEM of EZEKIEL is to be about *nine miles* in length and nine in breadth; covering an area of about *eighty-one square miles*. But the NEW JERUSALEM is to measure *twelve thousand furlongs*, or *one thousand four hundred miles*, in length, and the same in breadth; covering an area not far less than *two million square miles*. Again: THE JERUSALEM OF EZEKIEL is to have a vast *Temple* within its walls, wherein the service of the Lord is to be carried on continually. But THE NEW JERUSALEM is to have *no Temple whatever*, but the Lord God Almighty and the Lamb are " to be " the Temple of it." Again: THE JERUSALEM OF EZEKIEL is to be refreshed by a *stream of water issuing forth from under the threshold of the house* eastward, and flowing into the straits which will unite the Dead Sea with the Mediterranean,[1] and upon the banks of these straits "shall grow all trees for meat, whose leaf shall not fade, ... and the fruit thereof shall be for meat, and the leaf thereof for medicine (bruises and sores)." But THE NEW JERUSALEM is to be adorned with "*a pure river of water of life*, clear as crystal, *proceeding out of the throne of God and of the Lamb*. In the midst of the street of it, and on either side of the river" is to be "*the tree of life*" bearing "twelve manner of fruits," and yielding "her fruit every month," and the leaves of the tree are to be for the service ($\epsilon\iota\varsigma$ $\theta\epsilon\rho\alpha\pi\epsilon\iota\alpha\nu$) of the nations. And once again : the *materials* of the JERUSALEM OF EZEKIEL are to be, for anything that appears to the contrary, of *ordinary* although *excellent kind*. But THE NEW JERUSALEM is to be built of *gold* and *precious stones*, with *gates of pearl*.

We cannot then confound these cities with each other. They are perfectly distinct. The one is to be *earthly*, the other *heavenly*. The one is for *time*, the other for *eternity*. Yet we cannot fail to observe points of similarity, sufficient both in number and strength, to lead us to conclude that in the Millennial Jerusalem of Ezekiel we have a *type* of that which shall come down from God out of Heaven.

Let us glance at one or two assertions which direct our

[1] See Chapter VI., page 165, etc.

thoughts towards THE NEW EARTH *generally*,—that earth
of which the Heavenly City is to be the capital.

The earth is to be gloriously peopled with "THE
NATIONS OF THEM WHICH ARE SAVED." Righteousness
and glory will reign everywhere. The glory of God
and of the Lamb, which is to be the brightness of the
New Jerusalem, will illuminate also the remotest
regions, so that their inhabitants will "walk in the
light of it." Surely, it will not be said to contradict
the received view concerning the eternal state, if we
thus suppose that *nations*, with their *kings and divers
orders of authorities and powers*, will then exist. Perhaps
some persons may be inclined to think it does. But
certainly the Bible leads us to believe that *it will be
so* nevertheless. "The *nations* of them which are saved,"
and the "*kings of the earth*," are spoken of in plainest
terms, as being coexistent with the NEW JERUSALEM,
and as bringing their glory and honour into it.[1] Indeed,
to think it would be otherwise, would be to think that
the order of things in the New Earth will be different
from that which has (so far as the Inspired Word
teaches us) existed in any part of the Lord's kingdom,
and to contradict all analogy. How frequently we read
about the "principalities and powers in heavenly places,"
the "thrones" also, and "dominions,"—the archangel,

[1] Rev. xxi. 24-26.

crowned elders, angels, seraphim! There is evidently
a diversity of order and power among those who have
their part in realms of glory. *There* are the great ones
bearing rule, and *there* are those who bow beneath their
sway. Nor can this orderly arrangement in a kingdom
where no sin exists disturb the happiness of any; but
the opposite; it needs must minister to the increased
happiness of all. For ourselves, shall we *complain,*
if on the throne of that celestial nation in which our
everlasting dwelling may be fixed, the Crown of Government be borne by Paul or Peter, James or John? Nay,
shall we not *rejoice* exceedingly concerning this, and
yield them gladly the obedience which is due? And
what if Mark, or Timothy, or Barnabas, or Silas, occupy
the seat of honour *next* in rank or authority,—shall we
oppose our voice? or shall we think that there will
therefore be unreasonable dealing on the part of God
towards us? Nay, do we not *ourselves*, as taught
by our Redeeming Lord, look forward to possess
authority? If we have wrought for Him with long
and earnest service, using well the talents which the
Lord has given us, do we not expect accordingly to
have dominion over *ten*, or *five*, or *two* cities, as the
case may be?

It is remarkable that so many people should be
strongly impressed with the idea, that in "THE WORLD

TO COME " all things will be *ethereal :* that our future resting-place will rather be *a space* wherein our happy spirits may fly here and there in glory, than a true *substantial world,* where men in actual bodies may abide and carry on such works as shall be found consistent with their glorified estate.

Certain it is from the Word of God, that every redeemed soul is to be clothed, before he enters on his heavenly glory, with *a body*—a substantial body; a body like that of our Lord in which He rose again; a body having flesh and bones.[1] That is to say, the very body which was dead and buried, is to be again assumed, but rendered *incorruptible,* and meet for Heaven.

Our SAVIOUR's resurrection was the type of OURS. As *He* rose, so shall *we* rise. Thus the Apostle Paul teaches us, in the fifteenth chapter of the First Epistle to the CORINTHIANS,—" Now is Christ risen from the dead, and become the first-fruits of them that slept. . . . But every man in his own order: Christ the first-fruits, afterward they that are Christ's at His coming." But if so, then we need not try to explain away the clear assertions of the Scripture as to the *substantial nature*

---

[1] No mention has been made of *blood.* Indeed it is probable that our Saviour's risen body had no blood. It is written, "flesh and *blood* cannot inherit the kingdom of God." The presence of blood implies that which is corruptible (1 Cor. xv. 50).

of the New Jerusalem. The fact that there shall
be Nations with their Kings,—that there shall be
Christ's Table, at which the Redeemed shall eat and
drink with Him,—that there shall be Water of Life
and Trees of Life, of which the nations of God's
saved people may partake,—presents for our acceptance
no peculiar difficulty.   Do we not call to mind how Jesus
being raised again, took bread and fish, and an honey-
comb, and did eat before His wondering disciples?
How he entered into the house with two of them, and
sat there as beforetime, and took bread, and blessed it,
and brake, and gave to them?   Surely He was the
selfsame Jesus.   His hands and feet and side were witnesses of this.   And, except only when their eyes were
holden, His disciples *knew Him.   In this very body*, He
now sits enthroned above.   The " flesh and bones " with
which the Lord ascended are not found unworthy of the
Father's glory, nor inconsistent with the residence of
spiritual beings of the *highest* and the *holiest ranks.*
There is no objection, then, to things *substantial*, even
in the Heaven of Heavens!

If it be so, what room is there for hesitation?   We
are to be actually men, as truly so as we are now; *not
mere spirits,* for " a spirit hath not flesh and bones."
And why may not the earth, renewed, regenerated,
made free from the pollutions of iniquity by God's

all-purging fires, and formed again of such dimensions as shall be needful for the *multitudes* of the Redeemed,— be our eternal place of rest and glory? Why *must* we dwell on the idea that some far distant *star* or *space* above is to receive us when the Trumpet of the Lord shall sound for resurrection? True, we are to *meet* Christ "*in the air*" at first, and perhaps to enter with Him through the pearl gates of NEW JERUSALEM, and join His people at the marriage supper, while the city is suspended in the heights above. *But this will not be for eternity.* When JERUSALEM descends upon the new-created EARTH, it would appear that we are likewise to descend, and *earth*, adorned in new-born beauty, is to be our glorious abode. No roaring sea, no storms, no pestilence, no war, no misery, no sin, no Satan, no unholy flesh, are to disturb; but it will be EARTH no less, and men in actual bodies will inhabit it. What powers will be possessed by our renewed bodies, we are not informed. We only know that we shall be like Christ,[1] and that we shall "shine forth as the sun in the kingdom of our Father."[2]

Concerning *our position* in the New Earth, there are

---

[1] 1 John iii. 2.

[2] Matt xiii. 43; xxv. 21, 23, 34, 46; John xvii. 22, 24; 1 Peter i. 3, 5; Rev. vii. 13-17, etc.

one or two questions of deep interest which we must consider.

SHALL WE KNOW AGAIN THE FRIENDS WHOM WE HAVE LOVED IN THIS OUR LIFE OF SIN, AND LOVE THEM STILL WITH CLOSE ATTACHMENT AS OF OLD? Let us not hesitate a moment to reply, "UNDOUBTEDLY WE SHALL." *As* the disciples (except only when their eyes were holden) knew their risen Lord: *as* Abraham knew and spoke of Lazarus: *as* many from the East and West are to sit down with Abraham and Isaac and Jacob in the Kingdom of Heaven: *so* shall be the recognition. What did Paul mean but to declare this doctrine when he said, "I would not have you to be ignorant, brethren, concerning them which are asleep, that ye sorrow not, even as others which have no hope. For if we believe that Jesus died and rose again, even so them also which sleep in Jesus will God bring with Him. . . . . The dead in Christ shall rise first; then we which are alive and remain shall be caught up *together with them* in the clouds; . . . . wherefore *comfort one another* with these words."[1] Or when, again, the same apostle said, "What is our hope, or joy, or crown of rejoicing? are not even *ye*, in the presence of our Lord Jesus Christ, at His coming?"[2] What indeed had he in mind, unless it was the firm impression that in Heaven there would

---

[1] 1 Thess. iv. 13–18.   [2] 1 Thess. ii. 19, 20.

be a recognition amongst those who knew each other upon earth, and a continuance of that love which had united them so closely in their state of trial? No doubt there will be a recognition. No doubt the people of the Lord will carry on and perfect that attachment which on earth was found so sweet and so encouraging.

But then the question *will* arise, "Oh, what about those dear ones who will *not be found* in Heaven? those many parents, husbands, wives, children—loved,—yes, deeply loved,—but lost, because they would not have the Lord's salvation? Will it not be a fearful flaw in our eternal happiness—will it not for ever mar our glorious peace—to know that they are consigned to the unceasing flame of torment? *Will* it not? *Must* it not? It neither *must* nor *will*. THE MIND OF CHRIST, in that great day of *perfect righteousness*, will be *the mind of every saved soul*. The *feelings* of the regenerated flesh will not (like those of the unholy flesh which clothed the spirit formerly) resist the will and work of God. There will be then no law in the members warring against the law of the mind. The will, the love, the justice, of the Lord will be in absolute accordance with the desires of every inhabitant of the NEW HEAVEN and the NEW EARTH. What God shall have decreed, in that will every soul find pleasure. *No momentary wish* will be found passing through the heart of *the least Saint* in

bliss to alter what the Lord may have appointed, or to
change the state of any soul, except in full agreement
with 'His perfect will. The various decrees, therefore,
of the Day of Judgment, fixing, as they will have done,
the everlasting destiny of every child of man, according
to his works, will be precious in the sight of the
Redeemed. And though they had, in times gone by,
known fathers, mothers, husbands, wives, children, and
others, *after the flesh* (the flesh of *those* days, which could
love without regard to the Lord's holy will), yet now
they will know them no more. Nor will they *wish* to
know them. The decree of the Almighty will have been
passed concerning them, and it will be enough. The
Saved will have *no mind* to serve, except THE MIND OF
CHRIST, which then will reign as perfectly in all the
members of their glorious body as in their inner spiritual
man. It may be that in this present state, in which the
unregenerated flesh is charged with the affections which
are natural thereto, and which endear the parent to the
child, the husband to the wife, and friend to friend, it is
peculiarly difficult to comprehend how perfect happiness
can exist where the very closest ties of earth are to be
broken, and that for ever. But we must remember that
THE GREAT GOD, who is the GOD OF JUSTICE, but whose
NAME IS LOVE, has power and goodness which will prove
sufficient in this thing, as in every other. He will make

our heavenly minds to be in such entire conformity with His mind, that we shall find no cause for anything but *praise* by reason of *the most tremendous sentence* which His perfect justice will see fit to execute.

Will not also the same conformity of mind make every saint in bliss (the very *lowest*, just as truly as the *highest*) satisfied most perfectly with the particular place which, in accordance with the just decrees of the Great Day of Christ, he will be called to occupy?

I think, then, that the question which so frequently arises as to the unhappiness consequent upon the separation at the Great Day of Judgment, of so many who have dearly loved each other upon earth, and their consequent departure one from the other for eternity, has only weight by reason of our want of due consideration of the new *natural desires* which will be implanted in that mind when it is conformed entirely to THE MIND OF GOD.

But why should any one allow a doubt to rise within him upon any point concerning the true peace of the believer when he shall enter the eternal glory? Has not the Lord Jesus spoken plainly? Have not the Apostles and the Prophets borne their witness in the word of an unerring inspiration? Is it not clear by the unwavering testimony of God's Book of Truth— THAT THE RIGHTEOUS SHALL INHERIT EVERLASTING

HAPPINESS—THE JOY OF THEIR LORD—A PEACE, A REST, A STATE OF SATISFACTION IN WHICH NOT A FAULT SHALL BE DISCERNED, NOR ANY WANT EXPERIENCED? Is it not said that "the Lamb which is in the midst of the Throne shall feed them, and shall lead them unto living fountains of waters; and GOD SHALL WIPE AWAY ALL TEARS FROM THEIR EYES?" And shall we, in the face of all this testimony, think that there will be aught of misery in our blissful future? OH, NO! let us bid the thought for ever cease. It CANNOT BE. We have no choice but to look forward with rejoicing confidence to that estate of bliss which the NEW HEAVEN and NEW EARTH will in God's time reveal.

Thus have we introduced our readers—following, as we trust, the simple teaching of the Bible—through the eventful EVENTIDE of our poor fallen EARTH, to the bright dawn of the most glorious DAY of its REGENERATION. And here we find ourselves at the *last* point of information given in the Word of God. For the DAY, THE EVERLASTING DAY OF RIGHTEOUSNESS AND GLORY, is opened to our view, that we may enjoy, as it were, a momentary glimpse of its amazing wonders; —and the Inspired Volume closes.

And what need we more? LET US BUT PRESS ONWARD, CLOTHED WITH CHRIST, AND HAVING CHRIST

ABIDING IN OUR HEARTS; and those most precious things, of which it is not possible for man, thus burdened with unholy flesh, to speak, nay, which he cannot understand, will be laid open to our view; and by experience we shall learn their excellence, and before God REJOICE IN THEM WITH JOY UNSPEAKABLE AND FULL OF GLORY.

CHAPTER X.

Conclusion.

" Wherefore, beloved, seeing that ye look for such things, be diligent, that
ye may be found of Him in peace, without spot and blameless."

2 PETER iii. 14.

WE have been dealing, in the course of these pages,
with the deep things of the Divine Word. But
sincerely do I trust that they have not been
handled with presumption. Occasion has arisen frequently to refer to the *prophetic periods ;* but it will not
be said that we have spoken with unseemly positiveness
about the veiled future, as to days, and months, and
years. Those periods which have been sealed already
by the pages of *past* history, have been spoken of with
some degree of positiveness ; others have been referred
to with no other object than that of strengthening our
watchfulness by the offer of an extra point of *probability.*

Very much, however, which has been advanced in
the foregoing pages may have appeared *strange* to those
who have been used to entertain with strictness the
more ordinary views concerning the prophetic writings.

If what has been advanced has not convinced these persons, I would only say, let us not be too severe one towards another, because we see things, perhaps, from different points of view; but rather let us *pray for one another*, and for the whole Church of Christ, that God may grant each member thereof the spirit of a right discernment. *If God's children disputed less and prayed more, it would be far better.* There would be more light, more wisdom, more faith, more love, more peace, more holiness.

The object of this work has been to excite, if possible, amongst our fellow-believers *a more earnest and diligent study of the Scriptures, and a more constant watchfulness and unwavering preparedness for the Coming of our Lord.* There has been no endeavour to arouse an undue curiosity, nor to satisfy the minds of those who love to speculate upon "the times and the seasons, which the Father hath put in His own power." If, then, our God will make this little work a means of comfort or of strength to any of His people, or if He will so bless it with His Spirit, that it may be the instrument of awakening one poor unsaved soul, the object will be gained.

We have considered some of the most important subjects which the Bible has presented to the mind of the Christian. Many things connected with these subjects have an intimate concern both with the *present* and the *past*, but all of them bear strongly upon the *future*, and with urgency exhort each one of us— "PREPARE TO MEET THY GOD."

As we have dwelt upon the several points of moment one by one, we cannot fail, I think, to have discerned the fact that we must be approaching very near to the Great Day when Christ shall call His people hence. *How* near, we have not presumed to ask. But *near*, *very* near, *so* near, that the *waiting, watching* attitude is that which comes before us as the only safe position for a man on earth. AT ANY MOMENT (if what we have gathered from the Word of God is to be rested on), THE GREAT ARCHANGEL'S VOICE MAY SOUND, FOR ALL THE DEAD IN CHRIST TO RISE, AND ALL THE RIGHTEOUS LIVING TO BE CHANGED. For what remains yet unaccomplished? Surely, if it be true that in so marvellous a manner many are running to and fro, and knowledge is increasing, (which was the one great sign of "the end" God gave to Daniel;[1]) if also, the everlasting Gospel has been preached to every nation, *for a witness :* if the eighth Headship of the Roman empire—"the Beast that was, and is not, and yet is"— have been seated on the throne : if many be running to and fro, and knowledge be increasing : if the children of

---

[1] Dan. xii. 4.

Judah be prepared to take a fresh possession of their promised land, and the land be even now in readiness for such possession, and there need nothing but a hand of power and will to lead them back:—then *certainly* THE TIME IS SHORT: wherefore there is necessity to stand at once and constantly upon the watch-tower; and there is a loud and urgent call for prayer, for clothing with God's panoply, and for firm and constant walking in the love of Christ.

Nay, more—for even now, THE EVILS OF THE LAST DAYS give us warning of their quick approach, and lift their voice on high, that every one who values his immortal soul, and is concerned about the glory of the Lord, should put his armour on, and stand forth ready for the fight.

What means this INFIDELITY sitting in high places, calling itself *Christ's religion*, and gaining hearing with the educated people of the world, exercising marvellous control over the minds of those towards whom we look as future pastors of our churches and educators of our youth? What means the no less evil and increasing sway of so-called "SPIRITISM," which puts forth its creed, undermines in the most subtle way the truths of Holy Writ, and leads away its thousands upon thousands from the truth? What means that "BROAD," unholy doctrine, which gives one hand to the Roman harlot, and the other to the false churches of the East, and proclaims Heaven to be the resting-place of all people, so that they be only *earnest*, of whatever sects besides? What means that spirit which professes to hold fast by the Inspired Word, and speaks of *Christ* but *no Atonement, Heaven* but *no Hell?* What mean these strange minglings of good and evil, right and wrong, which, unrebuked, are found on every side? Do they not seem to bid us mark for probability that THE TIME IS SHORT?

But not only do these heresies abound, and do their work as mighty instruments of Satan, making many sad whom God has not made sad, and causing many to fall grievously who did run well, but iniquity of life abounds and grows amidst increasing light.

DRUNKENNESS, which slays its thousands upon thousands (seventy thousand, even in our own dear *Christian* nation, annually), while no less than £150,000,000 of our British money is taken from the hand of industry and spent in the accursed drink. FORNICATION, the extent of which is terrible in every land. SABBATH-BREAKING, FRAUD, DECEIT, abounding everywhere.

What can we say to these things? Will God suffer that His Name and Word shall be despised so greatly for any long extended period? Most surely He will not. Do but look upon our great advantages; our light; our knowledge; the education among rich and poor; the distribution of the Scriptures in the mother tongue of every nation, through the length and breadth of the earth; and then observe the state of fearful sin and darkness in which such multitudes of men are living; hearing, knowing, understanding, but *resolved to live in sin.* Surely the time *must* be short. It must be even now an *advanced hour* in this "EARTH'S EVENTIDE."

BUT IF SO, THEN DOES AN ESPECIAL DUTY LIE UPON EVERY CHILD OF GOD, BOTH TOWARDS

"THE WORLD AND THE CHURCH,"

that he let his light shine brilliantly and with a steady flame before the *one,* and that he walk in holy fellowship with the *other.*

THE WORLD "lieth in wickedness," and "passeth away."[1] Let every Christian see that he behave before it as a Christian *should* behave; bearing the cross; fearless of reproach; knowing how to speak a word in season both in wisdom and in love.

THE CHURCH has enemies outside her pale, and within her bosom. It is her day of *trial.* Her members, therefore, must both *pray* and *act in fellowship.* They must have a care for one another, such as their close

---

[1] 1 John v. 19, and ii. 17.

brotherhood demands; bearing in mind always the temptations and infirmities of *weaker* brethren, and leading them with tender, loving hands; feeding them with spiritual things, in wisdom and with prayer: the *elders* taking heed that none can find occasion to note *appearances* of evil in their walk and conver ation. Moreover, let that member of the Church who "thinketh he standeth, take heed lest he fall."

AGAIN: ON EVERY WAITING SERVANT OF THE LORD, THERE LIES RESPONSIBILITY OF NO INDIFFERENT KIND, RESPECTING

"ISRAEL AND ANTICHRIST."

"Pray for the peace of JERUSALEM; they shall prosper that love thee." As Israel's sons are looking towards their land, God's Gentile people must be ready to give help, when help is needed. Never must they be unmindful of the debt they owe—under God—to Israel, of whom, as concerning the flesh, Christ came. For the *Conversion* of "the Remnant," for the *Restoration* of the Kingdom, and for the *Salvation* of "all Israel," must their constant prayer be made, and ready help afforded.

Moreover, knowing what the Jewish people are to suffer at the hand of ANTICHRIST, and remembering how all *other* nations likewise are be bound up in their

affliction, it behoves God's people everywhere, to bear
"*that wicked one*" in memory before the Lord, and pray
that his dread hand of persecution may be stayed;
and plead the promise given, that "for the elect's
sake" the time of trial may "be shortened." And
besides this, seeing how the multitudes of earth will
be seduced by the usurper's subtlety, or driven to unjust
compliances by his extended rod of persecution; it is
incumbent on every servant of the Lord to keep the eye
of faith fixed *singly* and *firmly* on the Redeemer, JESUS
CHRIST; to hold fast by the WORD OF INSPIRATION;
to allow nothing to obtain a footing in his creed, but
that which is *revealed clearly* in the BIBLE; to suffer
no opinions, works, or systems, put forth by any man,
however high in public estimation, to interfere with
a simple resting upon CHRIST, and CHRIST ALONE; no,
nor even to obtain the slightest shadow of regard, unless
they *accord absolutely* with the teaching of the HOLY
BOOK OF GOD. "PROVE ALL THINGS; HOLD FAST
THAT WHICH IS GOOD." "PROVE," by the *Bible*; "HOLD
FAST," *by the Spirit*; doing every thing with Prayer.

AGAIN: THE SHORTNESS OF OUR TIME CALLS LOUDLY
UPON EVERY MAN, AND BIDS HIM BEAR IN MIND THAT
WHEN THE DAY OF ANTICHRIST SHALL BE AT HAND

"THE ADVENT"

OF THE SON OF MAN WILL BE REVEALED. To this,

T

the mind of every earnest Christian is directed, for he knows that it will be his introduction into everlasting rest.

ARE YOU, DEAR READER, LOOKING FOR THAT ADVENT? O remember what an awful matter it will be, when " one shall be taken, and the other left," to be among the multitude who shall be " *left !*"

But we will not suppose that there is any doubt concerning this. You are (we will believe), like every faithful servant, waiting for your Lord's appearing. Yet we must not be unmindful of the Adversary's subtlety, nor of the law of evil still abiding in the mortal flesh. Therefore it will not be wrong to urge on you, —" *Be diligent,* that you may be found of Him in peace, without spot and blameless." Beware, then, of lukewarmness. Shun all promptings to a carnal or a worldly spirit. Be decided, bold, determined ; and yet humble, meek, and prayerful. Think not that *the foot of the cross* is a place too low for the decided Christian.

Humble yourself often there, although, through union with your Lord, you sit in Him " in Heavenly places." And kneeling there in heart, with faith and love look up, look where you will, even to the right hand of God, and see a seat upon the Saviour's throne prepared for you to occupy. The Cross! How lowly, yet how blest a station! In that Cross is concentrated the great

ALL IN ALL of the immortal soul's salvation. To hold
by it is to be free from condemnation everlastingly.

BUT AGAIN : THE LORD DESCENDING TO THE EARTH,
WILL INSTITUTE THE FIRST PREDICTED ACT OF THE
GREAT JUDGMENT DAY,

"THE JUDGMENT OF THE NATIONS."

For this, His descent in glory will be "WITH HIS
SAINTS." Let Christians note this well. They who
shall have been caught up to meet the Saviour Jesus in
the air, shall come again with Him, when He descends
to "judge the nations righteously" and introduce His
reign. But if it will be so, and we are to form part
of the Almighty's awful train, "when every eye shall
see Him, ... and all the kindreds of the earth shall
wail because of Him"—"what manner of persons ought
we to be in all holy conversation and godliness?"

AND AGAIN, WHEN THIS FIRST ACT OF THE LORD'S
JUDGMENT SHALL BE NUMBERED WITH THE GREAT
EVENTS PASSED BY, AND

"THE REIGN OF RIGHTEOUSNESS AND PEACE"

SHALL HAVE BEEN INTRODUCED,—HOW HAPPY FOR THIS
FALLEN WORLD! Yet far more blissful than the state
of any who shall then be born into this world, will be
that of the vast multitudes who *now* (in our day) living
in this world, are really Christ's! They will have

entered on the morning of that glorious "FOR EVER
WITH THE LORD," — that wonderful abiding in the
presence of the King of kings; that indissoluble
union of the members of His Body, which shall
be the portion of believers when the Lord shall reign.
Then they shall know the fulness of that word which
had encouraged them so often while on earth,—" *If we
suffer we shall also reign with Him.*"[1]

AGAIN: BEYOND THE HAPPY PERIOD OF THE
SAVIOUR'S REIGN WE LOOK, AND SEE THE GREAT
DECEIVER, SATAN, LOOSED FROM PRISON, AND

"THE FINAL OUTBREAK OF EVIL"

ENSUE SPEEDILY. But we look forward to this last
grand effort of iniquity with no feelings of alarm on
the behalf of any. Instant and glorious will be the
shout which will echo through "the camp of the saints"
and through the "Holy City,"—the shout of triumph
and of praise. For in a moment will the power of God
arise, and before one of the true servants of Immanuel
can be hurt by the assaulting foe, the hosts of Gog and
Magog will be overthrown by fire from Heaven. We,
if we are Christ's, shall see the work, and join in that
grand shout of praise, the signal for the Break of the
ETERNAL DAY, the commencement of earth's pure and

[1] 2 Tim. ii. 12.

sinless state and the entire removal of iniquity from the sight of the Redeemed.

Let us dismiss this matter with a serious lesson. We find "*a thousand years*" *of punishment* are not sufficient to subdue the thirst of Satan after human souls. Then how can any child of man, while yet on earth, expect to remain free at any time from his assaults? What need we have to watch and pray against his power and subtlety! What need to seek sufficient strength from God, wherewith to meet and faithfully resist him! Remember DAVID, HEZEKIAH, PETER; these were *strong* men *overthrown*. Now, "if any man lack wisdom, let him ask of God, who giveth to all men liberally, and upbraideth not, and it shall be given him."[1]—God will "give His Holy Spirit to them that ask Him."[2] "As thy day, so shall thy strength be."[3]

AGAIN: WHEN ALL THE VOICE OF WICKEDNESS IS HUSHED IN DEATH BY REASON OF THE FIRE OF GOD, AND WHEN THE ARCHANGEL'S BLAST HAS SOUNDED THROUGH THE EARTH AND SEA, AND

"THE GENERAL RESURRECTION OF THE WICKED"

HAS ENSUED, AND ALL THE RIGHTEOUS LIVING ALSO, WHETHER IN THE HEAVENS OR ON EARTH, ARE SUMMONED TO THE GREAT WHITE THRONE OF JUDGMENT; NOT

[1] James i. 5.   [2] Luke xi. 11-13.   [3] Deut. xxxiii. 25.

A FEAR WILL CLOUD THE BROW OF ANY BABE IN CHRIST. The feeblest saint who ever bent the knee in prayer, the most hesitating of believers, will glory in a perfect confidence; for there will be no *mingling of sheep and goats* before that awful Throne of Majesty. The King shall place "the *sheep* on His *right* hand, and the *goats* on the *left*." Then let the trembling, doubting, but still *praying* one, take courage. Is he a *believer?* Then he shall be on the *right hand* of the Throne, and SAFE beneath the smile of the Eternal Judge. It may be, doubts and fears distress his spirit in these earthly days, but they can interfere in no wise with his safety. He feels, perhaps, his utter helplessness, he mourns over the weakness of his faith, he views with horror all the inconsistent actions of his Christian life, and goes on in a chastened spirit through earth's pilgrimage; but here is a great secret which should give him comfort— "NEVERTHELESS, THE FOUNDATION OF GOD STANDETH SURE." The shipwrecked sailor may be weak and helpless; but if by some kind hand of strength he has been landed on a rock, his weakness is of very slight account; the rock is *firm* and *high enough* above the waves, therefore he need fear no evil. If the ROCK BE SAFE, HE TOO IS SECURE. Let patience only do her perfect work. The storm will surely pass ere long, and friendly hands will bear him home.

AND ONCE AGAIN: THE NEW HEAVENS AND NEW EARTH WILL BE CREATED; AND THE MOST GLORIOUS CITY, "NEW JERUSALEM," THE CENTRE OF THE NEW EARTH'S PEACE, WILL DESCEND FROM GOD. Here shall the believer rest, and commune with his Lord and with the holy angels who have known no sin, and he shall weep no more. O READER, CAN YOU SAY THIS HEAVENLY HOME SHALL BE YOURS? Can you *feel your footing* on the ROCK OF AGES? and are you abiding thereupon while all the storms of sin and care are passing over? If it be so—O forget it not— FROM HENCE YOU SHALL BE BORNE TO THIS ETERNAL HOME. Happy they who find their rest upon this ROCK! What peace they have! Though it be faint, yet, O how sweet a foretaste of that bliss to be revealed in New Jerusalem! Would that all men who declare themselves "Believers" did in truth possess it! But, alas! how can they have it when they seek for it in such vain places and in such unseemly manner? See how they look for peace in their religious systems, churches, sacraments, services, charities. See how they seek for it arrayed in their own righteousness; or trusting to God's Mercy, altogether heedless of His Justice; or comparing their own excellence with that of others, and so claiming peace, as if of right. Alas! for them. There is *no peace* for any who thus seek it. They are but "like the troubled sea, when it cannot rest, whose waters cast up mire and dirt." "The way of peace have they not known." Peace is laid up IN CHRIST. In Him, and in Him only, can men find it. When a sinner beholds Him—his Substitute, who has borne his iniquities, carried his sorrows, washed out his guilt, and made full atonement, so that the Divine Justice of the Triune God is entirely satisfied —then, but then only, he has PEACE, *precious, glorious, lasting* PEACE. "BEING JUSTIFIED BY FAITH, WE HAVE PEACE WITH GOD, THROUGH OUR LORD JESUS CHRIST."

In NEW JERUSALEM, at the bright dawning of the EVERLASTING DAY, which shall succeed the EVENTIDE through which our earth must pass, do I sincerely pray that God may grant that those into whose hands this book shall fall, may find their GLORIOUS INHERITANCE, and, in the glad possession of its blessings, sing the praises of the Lamb in that "NEW SONG" which the Redeemed alone can sing; and with a voice, attuned to heaven's harmony, unite with the "ten thousand times ten thousand, and thousands of thousands," who shall be gathered round the throne of the Almighty King, to render with eternal joy the foretold adoration, "WORTHY IS THE LAMB THAT WAS SLAIN, TO RECEIVE POWER, AND RICHES AND WISDOM, AND STRENGTH, AND HONOUR, AND GLORY, AND BLESSING."

LONDON: S. W. PARTRIDGE & CO., 9, PATERNOSTER ROW.

NEW WORKS AND NEW EDITIONS

PUBLISHED BY

S. W. PARTRIDGE & CO.,

9, PATERNOSTER ROW, LONDON.

The SALOON SHOW ROOM is open daily from Nine till Six, Saturday till Two.

The Temperance Bible Commentary; giving at one view, Version, Criticism, and Exposition, in regard to all Passages of Holy Writ, bearing on 'Wine' and 'Strong Drink,' or Illustrating the Principles of the Temperance Reformation. By F. R. Lees, Ph. D., and Dawson Burns, M.A. Fifth edition, with Supplement. Demy 8vo., cloth, 6s.

Earth's Eventide, and the Bright Dawn of the Eternal Day. By Rev. J. G. Gregory, M.A., Incumbent of Emmanuel Church, Hove, Brighton. Fifth Edition. Fcap. cloth, 5s.

Sire and Son : a Startling Contrast. (A Temperance Tale.) By Rev. Amos White. With Engravings. Crown 8vo., cloth, 3s. 6d.

The Sabbath made for Man. Being the Essay awarded an Extra Prize by the Adjudicators of the Lord's-Day Observance Society. By Rev. G. A. Jacob, D.D. Crown 8vo. Paper, 1s. Cloth, 1s. 6d.

A Catechism on the Second Advent; and the Revealed Future of the Church and the World. By Rev. J. I. Jones. Fcap. 8vo., paper, 1s. Cloth, 1s. 6d.

Ben Owen; a Lancashire Story. By Jennie Perrett. Second edition. With Engravings. Fcap. 8vo., cloth, 1s. 6d.

Into the Light. By same Author. With engravings. Fcap. 8vo., cloth, 1s. 6d.

The Existence of Evil, considered in its Relation to the Divine Sovereignty. With Supplement on the Divine Fatherhood. By A. Medwin. 16mo., cloth, 1s.

Daily Thoughts for the Little Ones. By Mrs. F. J. Kershaw. Royal 16mo., limp cloth, 1s.

Prevailing Prayer; or Triumphant Faith, as seen in the Life of John E. Vassar. Illustrated with 16 Page engravings. Crown 8vo., cloth, 2s. 6d.

Neville Hatherley, a Tale of Modern English Life. By a Lady. With Introduction by the Rev. Stenton Eardley, B.A. Crown 8vo., cloth, 3s. 6d.

The Great Pyramid : its History, Scientific, Sacred, and Prophetic Teachings. By T. Septimus Marks. With Diagram. Second Edition. Crown 8vo., cloth limp, 1s. 6d.; boards, 2s.

The Closing Days of Christendom as Foreshadowed in Parable and Prophecy. By Burlington B. Wale, Author of "Biblical Outlines," &c. Crown 8vo., cloth, 5s.

Seven Men. By the Countess de Gasparin. Adapted to the English. Introduction by J. M. Weylland. Frontispiece. Crown 8vo., cloth, 1s.

Songs under His Shadow. Original and Translated. By Mrs L. T. C. Crown 8vo. cloth, 2s. 6d.

The Apocalyptic Histories : in Plain Language, and Chronologically arranged into one Diagram. With Supplementary Notes. By the Author of "Life in Christ." Demy 8vo., cloth, 5s.

Memorials of Temperance Workers; containing Brief Sketches of nearly One Hundred deceased Labourers. By Jabez Inwards. Crown 8vo., cloth, 5s.

Ritualism : Romanism : and the Reformation : a Question of Fact. By Samuel Wainwright, D.D., Author of "Christian Certainty," &c.   Large Post 8vo., cloth, 7s. 6d.

Confession : a Doctrinal and Historical Essay. By L. Desanctis. Translated from the Eighteenth Italian Edition by the Rev. M. H. G. Buckle, Vicar of Edlingham. Crown 8vo., cloth, 3s. 6d.

Christ and full Salvation.   By Rev. J. B. Figgis, M. A.   Second Edition. Fcap. 8vo., cloth, 2s. 6d.

Light in the Liturgy. By Maria Sandberg, Author of "Glimpses of Heaven," &c. Second Edition.   Demy 32mo., cloth, 1s.

The "Fear Nots" of Scripture ; or, Apples of Gold in Pictures of Silver. By Miss Catherine M. Mead. 16mo., cloth, 1s.

I Know ; or, the Verities of the Bible. By Mrs. Peploe, Authoress of "Naomi," &c. Second Edition. 16mo., cloth, 1s. 6d.

Cheering Words for Weary and Troubled Believers.   By Rev. Alfred Tyler. Second Edition. 16mo., cloth, 1s.

The People of Pentonby. A Temperance Story. By Miss Jessie M. Maxted. With Portrait of Mr. S. Morley, M.P., and Engravings. Crown 8vo., cloth, 2s. 6d.

Byway Gleanings. Contents : Sergeant Cotton—Sturt Fane—Rachel, the Petroleuse —Nitta. By Miss Fannie Surtees. Foolscap 8vo., bevelled cloth, 2s.

Witton's Main ; and other Stories. By the same Author. Foolscap 8vo., cloth, 1s. 6d.

Bric-a-Brac Stories. Contents : Sam—Good for Nothing—Trochard. By the same Author. Second Edition. 18mo., cloth, 1s. 6d.

Home-Spun Stories. Contents : Scoresby Quay—Will Wild, the Railway Guard— The Loss of the Steamers—"To your Health, Proctor"—The Raft. By the same Author. Third Edition. 18mo., cloth, 1s. 6d.

Martha the Merry ; or, As One Door Shuts another Opens. By Mrs. Jerome Mercier. Frontispiece. Crown 8vo., cloth, 1s. 6d.

Sebie Dorr ; a Dream of the Past. By Mrs. R. H. Surtees-Allnatt, Author of "Autumn Gatherings," &c. Crown 8vo., cloth, 3s. 6d.

Autumn Gatherings. I. Mabel Ashton, a Tale of the Crimean War. II. The Recluse of Rutherford Manor. By the same Author. Frontispiece. Post 8vo., cloth, 2s.

Coffee Taverns, Cocoa Houses, and Coffee Palaces: their Rise, Progress, and Prospects. By E. Hepple Hall, F.S.S. With Engravings. Crown 8vo., paper boards, 1s. ; cloth, red edges, 2s.

The Royal Priesthood ; or, The Power of an Endless Life. By Anne Maine. Author of "Light for the Dark," &c. Foolscap 8vo., cloth, 1s.

Stars of the Reformation : being short Sketches of the Reformers, &c.   By J. Milton Smith. Second Edition. With 8 page Engravings. Crown 8vo., cloth, bevelled boards, 3s. 6d.

Crumbs from Dame Nature's Table. By Mrs. Alfred W. Adams. Second Edition. With Engravings. Royal 16mo., cloth, 3s.

Sketches of Primæval History. By Rev. J. G. Gregory, M.A. Crown 8vo., cloth, 2s.

Memorials of the Wesley Family. By G. J. Stevenson, M.A. From Original Documents, and including Biographies of the Wesley Family for nearly 250 years ; with Genealogical Table from A.D. 938 to the year 1875. With Photographic Group of 15 Portraits. Demy 8vo., pp. 584, cloth, 12s. ; morocco, 16s.

Our Dear Eva ; or, Christian Childhood. By Author of "Jenny's Geranium," &c. Portrait. Royal 16mo., cloth, 1s. 6d.

Heathen England, and what to Do for it. By G. R. Paper, 1s. ; cloth, 2s.

Gilbert Wright, the Gospeller : a Tale of the Lollards. By F. S. Merryweather. With Frontispiece. Post 8vo., cloth, 3s. 6d.

Father Rutland ; or, the Ban of St. Peter. A Story of the Marian Persecution. By F. I. Tylcoat. Post 8vo., cloth, 2s. 6d.

The Hunchback of Carrigmore : an Irish Tale. By J. F. Scott. With Frontispiece. Post 8vo., cloth, 2s. 6d.

Eliezer ; or, Suffering for Christ. By Miss C. E. Stern. With Portrait. Crown 8vo., cloth, 2s. 6d.

Esther : a Tale of Modern Jewish Burgher Life. By the same Author. Crown 8vo., cloth, 3s. 6d.

The Seven Topics of the Christian Faith. A Manual of Theology, Orthodox and Unsectarian. By Rev. P. Maclaren. Crown 8vo., cloth, 3s. 6d.

The Threefold Gift of God ; or, Christ Jesus, the Object of Faith, Hope, and Love. By Rev. W. Haslam, M.A. Second Edition. Crown 8vo., cloth, 3s. 6d.

Personal Experience ; being Lectures on Bunyan's "Pilgrim's Progress." By same Author. Cloth, 2s. 6d.

Uline's Escape ; or, Hid with the Nuns. A Tale of the Reformation. By Mrs. A. Orr. With Illustrations. Crown 8vo., cloth, 3s. 6d.

The Ark of God : the Transient Symbol of an Eternal Truth. Being Vol. I. of the "City Temple Pulpit." By Rev. Joseph Parker, D.D. Crown 8vo., cloth, 7s. 6d.

Things you ought to Know about Yourself ; or, Sketches of Human Physiology. By R. T. Kaufmann. With Illustrations. Crown 8vo., cloth, 2s. 6d.

How to Live Well, and Save Twenty per Cent. on a Moderate Income. Paper boards, 1s.

Jennett Cragg, The Quakeress : A Story of the Plague. By Maria Wright, Author of "The Happy Village," &c. Illustrated. Crown 8vo., Cloth, 3s. 6d.

Jesus at Nazareth : The Earlier Chapters of the Great Life. A Monograph. By S. W. Partridge, Author of "Upward and Onward," &c. Crown 8vo. Cloth 3s. 6d. ; morocco, 8s.

Woodleigh Park ; or, The Power of Home. A Domestic Story. By Martha C. France. Preface by Mrs. Gordon. Second Edition. Frontispiece. Crown 8vo., cloth, 3s. 6d.

Caroline Street ; or, Little Homes and Big Hearts. by M. E. Ropes, Author of "Only a Beggar," &c. With Illustrations. Crown 8vo., cloth, 3s. 6d.

Maud's Boy, and other Tales. By Ina More, Author of "Twilight Stories." With Frontispiece. Crown 8vo., cloth, 2s. 6d.

Our Island Home Described. Its Chief Cities, Towns, and Ports, Railways, and Manufactures, Ancient and Modern. By B. R. Bartlett. Illustrations. Post 8vo., paper, 2s. 6d, cloth, 3s. 6d.

The Polyglot Daily Text-Book. A Text in English, French, German, and Italian, for Every Day in the Year. 32mo., cloth, 1s. 6d.

The Brandens ; or, Workers in a Neglected Service. By Eliza Hutchinson, Author of "Our Neighbour," &c. Illustrations. Crown 8vo. 5s.

Chapters in Irish History. By W. B. Kirkpatrick, D.D., Dublin. Second Edition. Crown 8vo., cloth 2s. 6d.

Lectures on Bible Difficulties. By Rev. G. D. Copeland, Walworth. Paper 1s. ; limp cloth, 1s. 6d.

Fanny Brown and her Honey-Bees. By Mrs. J. M. Tandy, Author of "Old Barnaby's Treasure," &c. Illustrated. Impl. 16mo., cloth, 3s. 6d.

The Knight of Dilham. A story of the Lollards. By Rev. A. Brown, B.A., Author of "The Last of the Abbots." 16mo., cloth, 1s. 6d.

The Banner Unfurled. Containing upwards of One Thousand Choice Selections from Christian Writers. Compiled by the Editor of "Gathered Grain." 5s.

The Sunbeam of Seven Dials, and other Stories of the London Poor. By M. J. Nicholson. With Illustrations. Royal 16mo., cloth, 1s. 6d.

The Two Babylons ; or, The Papal Worship proved to be the Worship of Nimrod and his Wife. With Sixty-one Illustrations from Nineveh, Babylon, Egypt, Pompeii, &c. By Rev. A. Hislop. Sixth Edition. 8vo., cloth, 7s. 6d.

Bye-Path Meadow. By E. Paxton Hood. Coloured Frontispiece. 8vo., 3s. 6d.

Blind Amos and his Velvet Principles ; or, Proverbs and Parables for the Young Folk. By the same Author. New Edition, 1s. 6d.

The Merchant of Haarlem. A Tale of King Philip's Reign in the Netherlands. Illustrated, 16mo., cloth, 1s. 6d.

The Martyr of Brentwood ; or, Three Hundred Years Ago. Second Edition. Illustrated. 16mo., cloth, 1s. 6d.

Eldol the Druid ; or, The Dawn of Christianity in Britain. Illustrated. 16mo. cloth, 1s. 6d.

Fiddy Scraggs ; or, A Clumsy Foot may Step True. By Anna J. Buckland. Frontispiece. Crown 8vo., cloth, 1s. 6d. (A Book for Servant Girls.)

Mick Tracy, the Irish Scripture Reader. With Engravings. Fifteenth Thousand. Crown 8vo., cloth, 3s. 6d.

Tim Doolan, the Irish Emigrant. By the same Author. With Illustrations. Fifth Thousand. Crown 8vo., cloth, 3s. 6d.

Gathered Grain; consisting of Select Extracts from the Best Authors. Fourth Edition. Crown 8vo., cloth, 3s. 6d.

Counsels and Knowledge from the Words of Truth. By the Rev. F. Whitfield, M.A. Second Edition. Crown 8vo., cloth, 3s. 6d.

Life Truths. By J. Denham Smith. 16mo., cloth, 1s. 6d. (People's Edition 6d.)

Life in Christ. By the same Author. 16mo., cloth, 1s. 6d.

Beads without a String. Brief Thoughts on Many Subjects. By S. W. Partridge. Author of "Upward and Onward," &c. Crown 8vo., cloth, 4s.; gilt, 5s.; morocco, 8s.

Upward and Onward. A Thought Book for the Threshold of Active Life. By the same Author. Eleventh Thousand. Crown 8vo., cloth 4s.; gilt, 5s.; morocco, 8s.

ILLUSTRATED BOOKS.

The Providence of God Illustrated. By the Author of "History in All Ages." Large crown 4to, cloth, 10s. 6d.

Jack, the Conqueror; or, Difficulties Overcome. By Mrs. C. E. Brown. 3s. 6d.

Our Picture Book. Small Folio. 600 Engravings. Paper, 5s.; cloth, 7s. 6d.

Cloudland; or, The Secret of Usefulness and Happiness. Fcap. 4to., cloth, 3s. 6d.

Arthur Egerton's Ordeal; or, God's Ways not Our Ways. By E. Leslie. With Full-page Engravings. Cloth, 3s. 6d.

Little Tot's Album. By Miss Tupper. With 130 full-page Engravings. Cloth, 5s.

Temperance Stories for the Young. By T. S. Arthur, Author of "Ten Nights in a Bar-room," &c. 2s. 6d.

Stories of Irish Life. By H. Martin. Royal 8vo., cloth, 3s. 6d.

Rag and Tag; or, A Plea for the Waifs and Strays of Old England. By Mrs. E. J. Whittaker. Crown 8vo., cloth, 1s. 6d.

A More Excellent Way; and other Incidents in the Women's Gospel Temperance Movement in America. Crown 8vo., cloth 2s. 6d.

Three People. A Story of the American Crusade. With 29 page Engravings. Crown 4to., cloth, 5s. Cheap Edition, paper, 1s. 6d.; cloth, 2s.

The Brook's Story, and other Tales. By Mrs. Bowen. An interesting Story for the Young. Cloth, 3s. 6d.

Our Four-footed Friends; or, The History of Manor Farm, and the People and Animals there. By Mary Howitt. With numerous Illustrations. Cloth, 3s. 6d.

The Bible Picture Roll. Containing a large Engraving of a Scripture subject, with a few lines of letterpress, for each day of the month. With coloured cover, 3s.

Gerard Mastyn; or, The Son of a Genius. By E. Burrage. Cloth, 2s. 6d.

Anecdotes for the Family. A Selection of interesting Anecdotes, suitable for the Social Circle. Crown 8vo., cloth, 3s. 6d.

Birdie and her Dog; with other Natural History Stories. Forty-one Illustrations. Cloth, 3s. 6d.

Stories about Horses. Compiled by the Editor of "The British Workman." Illustrated by Harrison Weir. Cloth, 5s.

Our Zoological Friends. By Harland Coultas. Cloth, 6s.

Music for the Nursery. Revised by Philip Phillips, the "Singing Pilgrim." A collection of fifty of the sweet pieces for the "Little Ones," that have appeared in the "Infant's Magazine," &c. With numerous illustrations. Cloth, 2s. 6d.

(Full Catalogues post free on application.)

LONDON: S. W. PARTRIDGE & Co., 9, PATERNOSTER ROW.

Trieste Publishing has a massive catalogue of classic book titles. Our aim is to provide readers with the highest quality reproductions of fiction and non-fiction literature that has stood the test of time. The many thousands of books in our collection have been sourced from libraries and private collections around the world.

The titles that Trieste Publishing has chosen to be part of the collection have been scanned to simulate the original. Our readers see the books the same way that their first readers did decades or a hundred or more years ago. Books from that period are often spoiled by imperfections that did not exist in the original. Imperfections could be in the form of blurred text, photographs, or missing pages. It is highly unlikely that this would occur with one of our books. Our extensive quality control ensures that the readers of Trieste Publishing's books will be delighted with their purchase. Our staff has thoroughly reviewed every page of all the books in the collection, repairing, or if necessary, rejecting titles that are not of the highest quality. This process ensures that the reader of one of Trieste Publishing's titles receives a volume that faithfully reproduces the original, and to the maximum degree possible, gives them the experience of owning the original work.

We pride ourselves on not only creating a pathway to an extensive reservoir of books of the finest quality, but also providing value to every one of our readers. Generally, Trieste books are purchased singly - on demand, however they may also be purchased in bulk. Readers interested in bulk purchases are invited to contact us directly to enquire about our tailored bulk rates. Email: customerservice@triestepublishing.com

You May Also Like

Characteristics of Christian Morality: Considered in Eight Lectures Preached Before the University of Oxford, in the Year 1873, on the Foundation of the Late Rev. John Bampton, Canon of Salisbury

I. Gregory Smith

ISBN: 9780649425327
Paperback: 164 pages
Dimensions: 6.14 x 0.35 x 9.21 inches
Language: eng

Researches on the Chemistry of Food

Justus Liebig & William Gregory

ISBN: 9780649692453
Paperback: 202 pages
Dimensions: 6.14 x 0.43 x 9.21 inches
Language: eng

www.triestepublishing.com

You May Also Like

ISBN: 9780649529377
Paperback: 126 pages
Dimensions: 6.14 x 0.27 x 9.21 inches
Language: eng

Vagabond Rhymes

Eliot Gregory

ISBN: 9780649037964
Paperback: 280 pages
Dimensions: 6.14 x 0.59 x 9.21 inches
Language: eng

A Doctor's Table Talk

James Gregory Mumford

www.triestepublishing.com

You May Also Like

ISBN: 9780649333158
Paperback: 84 pages
Dimensions: 6.14 x 0.17 x 9.21 inches
Language: eng

Report of the Department of Farms and Markets, pp. 5-71

Various

ISBN: 9780649324132
Paperback: 78 pages
Dimensions: 6.14 x 0.16 x 9.21 inches
Language: eng

Catalogue of the Episcopal Theological School in Cambridge Massachusetts, 1891-1892

Various

You May Also Like

ISBN: 9780649352142
Paperback: 88 pages
Dimensions: 6.14 x 0.18 x 9.21 inches
Language: eng

Three Hundred Tested Recipes

Various

ISBN: 9780649419418
Paperback: 108 pages
Dimensions: 6.14 x 0.22 x 9.21 inches
Language: eng

A Basket of Fragments

Anonymous

Find more of our titles on our website. We have a selection of thousands of titles that will interest you. Please visit

www.triestepublishing.com

Lightning Source UK Ltd.
Milton Keynes UK
UKOW01f1329231017
311488UK00017B/3688/P